Praise for

Culture Is Our Weapon

MAKING MUSIC AND CHANGING LIVES IN RIO DE JANEIRO

"In 1956, I was in Dizzy Gillespie's group touring Brazil with the United States State Department. While I was there, Venicius De Morales showed me the first favelas, which even back then had more than three thousand kids with no parents . . . now there are hundreds of thousands of kids living in favelas all over Brazil. No matter where you are in the world, the ghetto is the ghetto. I grew up on the South Side of Chicago during the Great Depression, and there was something uncomfortably familiar about visiting AfroReggae in Rio for the first time. But despite these difficult circumstances, AfroReggae's incredible talents for the work that they undertake truly inspired me. This book captures the energetic feel of the city and of everything Afro-Reggae does perfectly."

—Quincy Jones

"In documenting the rise of a unique NGO, Neate and Platt provide the best and most accessible account of life in Rio's favelas. And for once, it isn't all bad news."

—*The New Statesman*

PENGUIN BOOKS

Culture Is Our Weapon

PATRICK NEATE is the author of the novels *The London Pigeon Wars*, *City of Tiny Lights*, and *Twelve Bar Blues*, which won the Whitbread Novel Prize. His book *Where You're At: Notes from the Frontline of a Hip-Hop Planet* won the National Book Critics Circle Award for Criticism.

DAMIAN PLATT worked in the office of the International Secretariat of Amnesty International between 1997 and 2005, researching and campaigning against human rights violations in the Americas region. Between 2006 and 2008, he was the International Relations coordinator for AfroReggae. He is currently working to establish a cultural center in Morro da Providência, Rio's first favela.

CAETANO VELOSO is a musician, writer, and political activist who has been called the Bob Dylan of Brazil. He is most often associated with Tropicalismo, a musical movement that encompassed theater, poetry, and music, and which emerged in the 1960s, at the beginning of the Brazilian military dictatorship.

Culture Is Our Weapon

MAKING MUSIC AND CHANGING LIVES
IN RIO DE JANEIRO

Patrick Neate *and* Damian Platt

Foreword by
Caetano Veloso

PENGUIN BOOKS

PENGUIN BOOKS
Published by the Penguin Group
Penguin Group (USA) Inc.
375 Hudson Street, New York, New York 10014, USA
Penguin Group (Canada), 90 Eglinton Avenue East, Suite 700, Toronto, Ontario
Canada M4P 2Y3 (a division of Pearson Penguin Canada Inc.)
Penguin Books Ltd, 80 Strand, London WC2R 0RL, England
Penguin Group Ireland, 25 St Stephen's Green, Dublin 2,
Ireland (a division of Penguin Books Ltd)
Penguin Group (Australia), 250 Camberwell Road, Camberwell,
Victoria 3124, Australia (a division of Pearson Australia Group Pty Ltd)
Penguin Books India Pvt Ltd, 11 Community Centre,
Panchsheel Park, New Delhi—110 017, India
Penguin Group (NZ), 67 Apollo Drive, Rosedale, North Shore 0632,
New Zealand (a division of Pearson New Zealand Ltd)
Penguin Books (South Africa) (Pty) Ltd, 24 Sturdee Avenue,
Rosebank, Johannesburg 2196, South Africa

Penguin Books Ltd, Registered Offices:
80 Strand, London WC2R 0RL, England

First published in Great Britain by Latin Amercan Bureau 2006
First published in Penguin Books 2010

3   5   7   9   10   8   6   4   2

Copyright © Patrick Neate and Damian Platt, 2006
All rights reserved

LIBRARY OF CONGRESS CATALOGING-IN-PUBLICATION DATA
Neate, Patrick.
Culture is our weapon : making music and changing lives in
Rio de Janeiro / Patrick Neate and Damian Platt; preface by Caetano Veloso.
p. cm.
Orginally published : London : Latin American Bureau, 2006.
ISBN 978-0-14-311674-5
1. Blacks—Brazil—Rio de Janeiro—Social conditions.   2. Blacks—Crimes against—
Brazil—Rio de Janeiro.   3. Social problems—Brazil —Rio de Janeiro.
4. Social change—Brazil—Rio de Janeiro.   5. Non-governmental organizations—
Brazil—Rio de Janeiro   6. Rio de Janeiro (Brazil)—Social conditions.   I. Platt,
Damian.   II. Title.
F2659.N4N416   2010
306.098153—dc22   2009041080

Printed in the United States of America
Set in Sabon • Designed by Elke Sigal

Except in the United States of America, this book is sold subject to the condition that it shall not, by way of trade or otherwise, be lent, resold, hired out, or otherwise circulated without the publisher's prior consent in any form of binding or cover other than that in which it is published and without a similar condition including this condition being imposed on the subsequent purchaser.

The scanning, uploading, and distribution of this book via the Internet or via any other means without the permission of the publisher is illegal and punishable by law. Please purchase only authorized electronic editions, and do not participate in or encourage electronic piracy of copyrighted materials. Your support of the author's rights is appreciated.

Contents

Authors' Note

José Junior, founder and Executive Coordinator of Afro-Reggae, came to London in the spring of 2005 to plan AfroReggae's tour of the UK in March 2006. Junior had never been to London before and therefore contacted everyone he knew in advance. That included us. Damian had several dealings with AfroReggae while working as Amnesty Campaigner for Brazil, including helping out during 2004's invasion of the organization's parent favela (shantytown) by a neighboring drug faction. Patrick interviewed Junior and wrote extensively about AfroReggae in his book about global hip-hop, *Where You're At: Notes from the Frontline of a Hip-Hop Planet* (Riverhead).

We met in a swanky Soho bar and Junior was, as ever, full of ideas. He was concerned that AfroReggae shouldn't just play gigs but also transmit some of their ethos through discussions, workshops, and the like. Knowing AfroReggae's extraordinary work in Brazil, we were naturally enthusiastic—perhaps too enthusiastic. Because Junior produced his pointing finger—a gesture with which we've become all too familiar—and said it was vital that British people, in fact *all* people, understood the context in which AfroReggae works; the context of war in a nominally peaceful society. What was required was a book, he said, finger pointing, and we were the ones to write it. For both of us, it turned out to be the first manifestation of something we'd long suspected: You don't say no to Junior.

Consequently, we headed to Brazil in October 2005 to research the book you're now reading. Little did we know that we'd still be working on it the best part of five years later, or that AfroReggae would have come to play such a fundamental part in both of our lives. For Patrick, this has meant writing extensively about AfroReggae in the British media and several trips back to Brazil, most recently to write about the destruction of the Amazon rain forest and its communities. For Damian, however, it has meant a whole lot more. In 2006, Damian went to work for AfroReggae in Rio and has experienced firsthand many of the successes, failures, and ongoing contradictions that we write about in what follows.

Culture Is Our Weapon is a book about an NGO, certainly. But it is also a book about the strange, ignored, and frankly horrific war that's currently being fought in the beautiful city of Rio de Janeiro. Neither of us is an academic, so this is not an academic book. Rather it is a snapshot of the situation in Rio as it is now. Mostly, however, it is a book about potential, the potential that is released when people from violent, oppressed, and alienated communities seize space and find their voice. AfroReggae is an utterly remarkable organization that has a lot to teach us all. If you take nothing else from reading this, we hope you take that.

There are a couple of things we'd like you to bear in mind. First, we have occasionally chosen to use Portuguese words in the text. Sometimes, this is because the Portuguese holds a nuance that, we feel, defies translation and sometimes it's just because we think it reads better. All the Portuguese is, however, translated in either the text itself or the footnotes. Second,

AfroReggae works in an extremely dangerous environment. Therefore, some names have been omitted to ensure the safety of our friends.

Finally, it is our pleasure to thank the organizations and people without whom this could never have been written: the Arts Council and the British Council in Rio for their financial support, People's Palace Projects and the Latin American Bureau for their expertise and enthusiasm, Marton Merritt for his tireless translation, Caetano Veloso for his generous preface and all the people we interviewed from all walks of life who were uniformly eager and helpful. Damian thanks Amanda and Julian Platt for their support in London. Patrick thanks Francis and Patricia Neate for all their reading and notes. Lastly we must thank AfroReggae, both for inspiring this book and, most of all, for inspiring us.

Foreword

I am not from Rio de Janeiro originally but from a small town in Bahia, so I remember how, as a kid, we all used to look to this city for inspiration. It was, of course, the capital during the Empire and then the Republic, but it was also the cultural capital of Brazil. I remember going to the cinema in the 1950s and the images we'd see of the city: Copacabana Beach, Sugarloaf, Christ the Redeemer, samba, and Carnival. And, of course, the favelas.

It may seem hard to believe now but, traditionally, Rio is a city that has been proud of its favelas and all the cultural expressions that have emerged from them. São Paulo, for example, is different: the poor areas are a long way from the center, so rich and poor don't feel like they belong to the same town. But in Rio, many favelas are at the heart of the city and they've always been a source of pride for the whole population. In my teens, I remember sambas praising the particular beauty and happiness of favela life and later, in the 1970s, I often used to visit favelas like Mangueira myself. Even now, you'll find the richest and most chic families joining the samba parades because they're Cariocas* and they love to celebrate the culture. But these days something has changed.

---

* Cariocas are Rio natives.

Historically, the basic difficulty facing Brazil has always been the enormous disparity of wealth between rich and poor. All things considered, Brazil is a very convivial country but this huge poverty gap is an invitation to violence. Now add drug trafficking to that situation and see what happens.

I'm not an expert, but I guess it began in the early 1980s: people in the favelas began to deal cocaine and suddenly some of the poorest people became very rich and powerful. Suddenly they were dealing with large amounts of money and they were able to buy weapons, police, politicians, judges, and lawyers. Of course, the irony is that it never secures these people a bourgeois lifestyle. They may be rich and powerful but they can't leave the favelas for fear of their lives, and they usually die young. This is the reality.

In the past, even the criminals in the favela were seen as somehow charming. I recorded a version of the song "Charles Anjo 45" and, with the benefit of hindsight, I can see that this song is a landmark, a turning point. By the time we recorded "Charles Anjo 45," he was already a character who was saluted with gunshots. You see, Jorge Ben (who wrote the song) is from Tijuca and that was precisely the kind of place where this new kind of criminality was beginning to spring up.

It is true that, even now, the gangsters in Rio have some kind of charm, but the levels of violence and fear have changed beyond recognition because of the drug trade. These days, I'm sorry to say, people are afraid and the face of the city has been transformed. Look at the way all the buildings in Zona Sul are guarded by barriers, security devices, and armored cars. This situation of fear and violence is the one in which AfroReggae does their work.

I first came across AfroReggae when they were just kids playing percussion. I can't remember exactly when it was or who invited me, but I know it was 1993, because it was just after the police massacred twenty-one civilians in Vigário Geral and I knew this group had been put together in response to that horror. I saw them perform in a hotel not far from Ipanema and, on that first occasion, I was simply impressed by their innocence. At the time, they were just kids imitating percussion groups from Bahia; that's what they did at the very beginning, and that's how I got to know them.

Later, I discovered that it was Junior who'd put them together and that he'd done other work in these poor communities, including creating the newspaper *AfroReggae Noticias*. So I kept my eye on them and we began to interact, and a little later they asked me to be their official godfather, with the actress Regina Casé as their godmother.

Over the years, I have seen the progress of AfroReggae, and their development has been unbelievable. They have worked incredibly hard and are very serious about what they do, but they also work joyfully. I don't know much about the work of other NGOs, but I do know about music and they do it incredibly well.

There is still a lot of fabulous music coming from the favelas: samba, of course, but now *funk* and hip-hop, too. AfroReggae are closest to hip-hop, but they mix it with other things that other groups don't. It's not fusion; rather, they put different styles side by side and create contrasts. I admire the way they compose their music, creating cuts and edits as in a movie. It's beautiful and very modern. I believe AfroReggae is unique and I'm proud to be associated with them. To be honest, even if their ideology was wrong and they were not about helping people anymore, they'd still be interesting because they're an important band.

But AfroReggae is about helping people. As I got to know

them, so I got to know their community. They took me to
Vigário Geral and I learned a lot about the environment in which
they work and the war culture that is nurtured by the drug trade.
I have seen for myself very young children handling heavy weapons and it's still unbelievable to me. But AfroReggae? These guys
teach younger children how to play and, in doing so, they keep
them out of the trafficking. They have built houses of culture
and music right in the middle of all this violence.

There are not many reasons to be optimistic in Rio right
now. It is a complex situation in which violence and fear are
on the rise and nobody seems to have a solution. But even
amidst all these difficulties you can find some examples of
beauty and excellence that give us all hope. This is what Afro-
Reggae represents.

CAETANO VELOSO
Rio de Janeiro, November 2005

Culture Is Our Weapon

1

Living in a War Zone

Leida

"Even New Year's Eve isn't safe. There are fireworks but there are lots of *tiros*,* too. My husband and I like to go up on the roof to see the view over São Conrado, but before midnight we go down to my mother-in-law's because we know there'll be shooting. So we begin our celebration on top and then, at five to twelve, we come down and wait—because there are *moradores*† who've been hit by stray bullets at midnight.

"From inside the house you can't really watch anything at all. If you climb on a bathroom chair and peer out, you can just about see something. But even so, it's only taking a peek. You see some of the fireworks and they're pretty. But at the same time you see the tracer bullets flying to and fro and, in the end, you give up and try to get some sleep."

Leida is intelligent and unassuming, her manner exhibiting that quiet patience and dignity that so often seem to accompany a tough life. Six years ago, she left her family in the northeastern state of Maranhão to migrate south in the hope of

---

* *tiros*: bullets

† *moradores*: favela residents

finding a well-paid job. To an extent her wishes have been fulfilled. She works as domestic help for two households in the
asfalto* and earns a salary that, though a pittance by most
standards, is more than reasonable compared with those of the
northeast.

She has married a Carioca from Rocinha, one of Rio de
Janeiro's largest and most famous favelas. They live on the first
floor of her mother-in-law's house and, on weekends, her husband toils on the *laje*† building a second story. This upward
expansion is the most common manifestation of social mobility
in Brazilian favelas. If you can't, or don't want to, leave the
community, you construct more space for yourself and your
extended family by going up. Consequently, many of Rio's favelas are dotted with houses three, four, or even five stories high.
These are typically solid, colorfully painted buildings that boast
tiled verandas offering shade and a view. The common perception of favelas as crudely built shantytowns is often mistaken.

If Leida has ambitions for her home, she has ambitions for
herself, too. She doesn't want to spend her whole life getting
up at the crack of dawn to earn a tiny wage cleaning up after
the wealthy, and she's already spent a year and a half training
as a surgical assistant.

Her only access to such an opportunity was to pay for a
course herself, a course that takes six hundred hours to complete. Unfortunately, only those hours spent in the operating
theater count toward the qualification, and Leida had to pay
50 Reais‡ to the hospital each month for the privilege of her
training. She worked at night, slept between operations, and

---

* *asfalto*: literally "asphalt," used to refer to the city proper, where streets are
paved (as opposed to the favela, where they are not)

† *laje*: roof terrace

‡ One Real is currently, at the end of 2009, a little less than 57 US cents.

returned to her housekeeping jobs during the day. It was an impossible schedule and, in the end, she was forced to quit, but she still hopes to complete the remaining five hundred hours of her training someday.

The *cobertura*

It's a Saturday morning and we're sitting on the roof terrace of an apartment block in an affluent part of Rio, the hillside overlooking the world-famous Copacabana Beach District, fifteen minutes' walk from Avenida Atlántica. This is where we're staying.

After several days rushing around with an estate agent to be shown nothing but claustrophobic bachelor pads—all tacky décor and far too many mirrors—we finally got lucky. Aurélio, another northeasterner now living in Rocinha, led us to a bright, airy, and frankly enormous two-terraced penthouse that he looks after for its owner, a French theatre director. It happened to be available, and at a bargain price, too. The only condition was that Leida would come in every day to water the plants and make breakfast. No problem.

The flat is a *cobertura*—the chic, upper-middle-class equivalent of the *laje*—high on the eleventh floor. Paradoxically, however, the height of the penthouse setting actually sets us cheek by jowl with the neighboring favela and all its noise and activity. This is a typical Rio irony.

This favela, Ladeira dos Tabajaras, clusters around the road that winds its way up the hillside behind the building. Every morning is greeted by a chorus of barking dogs and crowing cockerels. But that's just the beginning of the daily racket. Saturdays, for example, are dedicated to blasting *forró* and *funk*,*

---

* *forró*: traditional accordion-based music from the northeast; *funk*: locally produced electronic dance music played at dances called *baile funk*

while Sunday nights are taken over by the thundering drums of the samba school: Its weekly practice sessions are becoming ever more enthusiastic in the months leading up to Carnival. Despite the refined surroundings of the *cobertura*, our ears belong to the favela.

One day at dawn, the dogs and cocks are drowned out by the sound of a helicopter that spends hours hovering over Tabajaras. It's a civil police machine overseeing some sort of operation on the ground. This is one of many such operations being carried out in the city in early November that are most likely related to the police killing of Bem-Te-Vi, the boss of drug trafficking in Rocinha. He was one of Rio's most wanted men.

Since Bem-Te-Vi's death, the police have undertaken a number of incursions into favelas dominated by drug factions that rival Amigos dos Amigos (ADA—Friends of Friends), the gang to which Bem-Te-Vi and, consequently, Rocinha belong. The purpose of these raids? To squash any plans by ADA's rivals to invade and take Rocinha and wrest control of its lucrative drug trade.

Over breakfast we read the news. Bem-Te-Vi's immediate successor, named in the newspapers as "Soul," has been killed by fellow members of ADA, the victim of an internal dispute— some "friends" they turned out to be. Rio's papers follow each step in the unraveling drama as if it were a soap opera, and the subplots come thick and fast: Bem-Te-Vi's *patricinha** girlfriend is arrested and photographed for the front pages. Rio's Public Security Secretary poses ghoulishly for the cameras, brandishing the dead drug lord's gold-plated Uzi. Most bi-

---

* *patricinha*: literally "Little Patricia," a tongue-in-cheek term for middle-class girls

zarrely, a group of men gathering *jaca* fruit cause panic in a road tunnel near Rocinha when motorists assume they are a gang of armed *traficantes*.* Dozens of cars are abandoned mid-tunnel, and the men are seized by the cops along with the sacks and knives they-were using to cut *jaca*.

The terrified atmosphere—all rumor and counter-rumor—owes much to concern that the death of Bem-Te-Vi will reignite last year's turf war between Rocinha and the neighboring favela of Vidigal. In April 2004, Dudu, head of trafficking in Vidigal, led some seventy men in an attempt to take over drug sales in Rocinha. Numerous civilians were killed during several days of fighting, first between the two factions, then between those two factions and the police, one thousand of whom were deployed in a belated attempt to control the violence. Dudu's attack took place two months after Rocinha residents petitioned the state authorities, saying they expected just such an invasion by traffickers from Vidigal any day. Their appeals for protection had been ignored.

Bulletins from the front line

Most mornings Leida provides us with an update from Rocinha, which we try to digest with our coffee and fresh papaya. Her calm testimony provides a fascinating and disturbing counterpoint to the newspapers' hyperbole. Today, for example, she describes the Sunday night they killed Soul, the way the shooting began in the upper half—*parte alta*—of the favela.

"We didn't know what was happening at first. I called my husband and we went to lie down on the floor in the kitchen. You're safer there because it puts two sets of walls between you

---

* *traficante*: drug trafficker

and the bullets. So we grab what we can and run to the kitchen. If there isn't enough time to get to the kitchen, we hide underneath the shower in the bathroom. It's a horrible feeling and nowadays it's happening more and more often.

"We heard them running past shouting, '*Vamos matar*,'* letting everyone know it wasn't the police. When I heard that, I shivered with fear because I thought it must be another invasion [by a rival faction]. From time to time the shooting stopped, then started again. It went on for an hour and a half. When we were almost asleep, we went back into the bedroom with our backs aching. We'd been in the kitchen for two hours in all."

Leida tells us that because of the internal dispute, people are saying that there are many members of Soul's group who've fled or gone into hiding. Her neighbor has a son who was affiliated with Soul, and he's disappeared. The other night ten *traficantes* went into this neighbor's house. Some of them were wearing masks, but the neighbor knew exactly who they were since they used to work alongside her son. She told them she didn't know where he was. They said that if they found him, he was dead. They claimed he owed them money and his mother didn't have enough to pay. "In the end," Leida says bluntly, "what they're doing is asking the mother for money not to kill the son."

As Leida talks, her eloquence grows and she gives a fascinating insight into life in the midst of Rio's drug war: "I'll never get used to living like this. I've been here for six years but, before the war, Rocinha was the favela where everyone wanted to live. It was peaceful—shoot-outs were rare and it was calm. You used to be proud to say you lived in Rocinha. Now I can't tell some people that this is where I come from.

"I have a friend I can't even go and see. She lives near here

---

* *Vamos matar*: "We're going to kill."

in Ladeira dos Tabajaras which is controlled by the Comando Vermelho,* and there's no way I can go to her house. If they find out I'm from Rocinha and they don't like it, they could beat her up or expel her from the favela. I'm even frightened to take a bus that goes past favelas run by other factions. If I want to meet my friend, we have to meet elsewhere; and I'm her daughter's godmother. She comes from Maranhão, too—people arrive from the northeast all the time. For everyone that leaves Rocinha, two arrive. When there's a war, people move out, rent out their houses, and so on. Other people move in and, if there's no fighting going on, they'll have the illusion that things will get better tomorrow."

As Leida tells her story there is a rapid series of loud bangs from the hillside behind the flat. It sounds like a dozen doors being slammed in quick succession. "*Tiros*," she says, lifting a finger in the air. There are a few moments of quiet and then— BANG BANG BANG BANG—the bullets are flying again. "They must be testing some new weapons." She shrugs and smiles. The automatic gunfire, directly level with the plush *cobertura*, continues intermittently for a few minutes.

"I don't think there's anything good about *o tráfico*.† You can't have a child, because you're scared they'll get involved. You can't keep an eye on them all the time—you'd have to keep them in the house and you'd both end up as prisoners. My husband and I have talked about it a lot but we're not ready for all that yet. For instance, your child goes to school but you don't know what happens on the way from school to the house because you're out at work. So your kid could become a *filho*

---

* Comando Vermelho: the "Red Command," Rio's oldest and biggest drug faction

† *o tráfico*: drug trafficking/the drug trade

do tráfico.* This happens a lot. You see ten-year-old kids with guns. A *traficante* might be in a bar, drinking and hanging out, and he'll give the kid a gun. And that kid feels like he's something. Then they'll ask him to run a message or deliver some money. The kid becomes an *aviãozinho.*† That's it, he's in.

"My mother-in-law has a grandson who is seven years old. It's frightening. Below my house, there's a little bar. One day a *traficante* called him over. Luckily my husband was there and he was able to say no. My husband grew up in Rocinha and he knows most of them. That's the only time it might be beneficial to know a *traficante*.

"Say one of them is rude to you, you can go to another one you know who can speak to the boss. And the boss will tell the rude guy that if he carries on behaving like that, he could die or be punished. So there's an advantage in knowing the *traficantes* in some situations but, even so, if they weren't there in the first place you wouldn't need to, would you?

"Many mothers are scared because of this. They're also scared of all the shooting and stray bullets. Their kids could be playing outside and all it takes is one bullet to finish someone's dreams. It must be very sad. And it's difficult for the mothers of traffickers, too. Because no mother wants her kid to get involved. The trafficker might get killed by the police, another faction, or even his own.

"My mother-in-law lost a son. He was killed by the guys he worked with. In fact, he'd already quit trafficking but he knew too much. So they came back and killed him, even though she'd been to the boss in person to ask him to forbid it."

We've told Leida why we're in Rio; that we're writing a

---

* *filho do tráfico*: child of the drug trade

† *aviãozinho*: literally "little airplane"; a runner or messenger

book about AfroReggae. Perhaps this is why she's so frank with us. She knows about AfroReggae and their work and she asks if it's true that their bands are made up of ex-*soldados*.* We tell her that, yes, some members of the bands and other people working in the organization did work in the *tráfico* in the past. Leida has one other question: "When they get out of trafficking and go into AfroReggae, do they manage to stay out?"

---

* *soldados*: soldiers, i.e., armed employees of the drug trade

2

The Cradle of Crime

History

There are more than six hundred favelas in Rio de Janeiro, housing around a third of the city's six million inhabitants.* In some ways they bear comparison with illegal shantytowns the world over, the inevitable by-products of urbanization as people from around the country seek employment in the big city—alienated communities both excluded from and exploited by the "city proper." In several crucial respects, however, the favelas reflect both the unique history—recent and long past—and the unique present of Rio and, indeed, Brazil.

To many people's continued anger, the favelas are permanent settlements. Sure, you will come across the occasional ramshackle slum that looks like it might blow away with the first breath of wind and, sure, many communities' sewer systems (or lack thereof) are far from ideal. But typically you're more likely to be struck by the sophistication of infrastructure than by its absence. Favelas, for example, have running water and electricity (in the overwhelming majority of cases pirated from the national grid) and are characterized by solid houses,

---

* As there are no official statistics for most favelas, estimates vary greatly.

longstanding businesses, and in some cases, a flourishing (presumably illicit) market in real estate.

Accepted history tells us that the first favela was Morro da Providência in the center of the city, which was colonized by a band of soldiers returning from the Canudos campaign in 1897. Fed up with waiting for free housing promised by the government, these soldiers built a community of their own.

Canudos, deep in the inhospitable interior of Bahia in the northeast of Brazil, was a settlement founded by a religious mystic known as Antônio the Counsellor, who gathered thousands of followers around him to declare independence from and resistance to the national government. It is somehow a very Brazilian irony that the remnants of the army that squashed Antônio the Counsellor's rebellion should have been the ones to found the first favelas: communities that, exactly like Canudos, are the direct consequence of state neglect.

Indeed, it is arguable that Rio's favelas are the best physical expression of the divisions at the very heart of Brazil: historical divisions between rich and poor, black and white, slave and slave-owner, and a native and African heritage juxtaposed with a European dream of modernity.

At the beginning of the twentieth century, the mayor of Rio, Pereira Passos, launched an ambitious redevelopment plan for the city. Nicknamed "The Tropical Haussman," Passos set about widening streets and knocking down unsanitary tenements in an attempt to rid the city of the epidemics (particularly yellow fever) that had long plagued it and create a modern and sophisticated capital worthy of the young republic.

But Passos's plans made no provision for Rio's working classes, a large number of whom were left homeless. What else could they do but take to the unwanted spaces, in particular the rocky outcrops that punctuate the landscape?

As is the case in all societies where the poverty gap is an unbridgeable chasm, the Brazilian state can be seen, both historically and today, as protector of the elite against the threat of the common man rather than protector of the rights of the individual. Only in Rio, however, do favelas loom above the city proper like cancers on its conscience.

These days, the most important characteristic of the favelas is that, in the absence of the state, almost everyone is controlled, supported, and exploited by one of the city's drug factions, highly organized criminal armies that have evolved since the late 1970s. And few favelas bear the scars of this relationship more obviously than Vigário Geral. Vigário was once the headquarters of Rio's oldest and biggest faction, the Comando Vermelho. It is also the birthplace of AfroReggae.

Vigário Geral

It's a couple of years since we last visited Vigário. Then, as we sped down the ramp from the highway, one of the most noticeable things was the graffiti on the walls, the way "TC" "TC" "TC" flashed by in green before giving way to the red "CV" "CV" "CV." Vigário sits right next door to another favela called Parada de Lucas, which is controlled by the Terceiro Comando faction. The two factions have been at war for more than two decades. The graffiti is gone now, though the war is far from over.

Last time, at the bottom of the ramp, we slowed to a crawl as we rolled into the favela. It was a dank afternoon and we switched on the car's inside light and wound down our windows so that we could be easily identified by the armed lookouts. The dirt streets were crowded and we rattled our way over crude speed bumps every few meters. These had been laid by the Comando Vermelho to ensure that no one got in or out too fast. We meandered around tight turns and through narrow alleys until we reached AfroReggae's center. We heard the syncopated rhythms of the drums and occasional bursts of raucous laughter long before we found the spot.

On this occasion, however, we barely decelerate as we turn into the favela. This is partly because a state initiative has finally replaced the bumpy tracks with level concrete and even subterranean drains, and partly because the car is being driven this time by JB, once a senior *traficante* in the Comando Vermelho, now a senior figure in AfroReggae. It is also because the streets are near deserted. In the last decade or so, the population of Vigário has fallen from something like 35,000 to closer to 9,000. This may be a poor community with little prospect of mobility, but nobody would choose to live in a war zone. And this is, by most definitions, a war zone.

JB's a tricky character to read. He has a ready smile and, beneath the peak of his baseball cap, his eyes are warm and easygoing. But, like all the *traficantes*, those still in the trade and those who've got out, he exudes a kind of preternatural calm. It's not that you can never tell what he's thinking, more that if he doesn't want you to know, you can be very sure you won't.

As we hustle through the narrow streets, JB greets everyone the same way, with an "All right, bitch" and a big grin. He is an ex-trafficker. He is a stalwart of AfroReggae. He is a pillar of the community.

A couple of the kids who raise their arms and laugh in response are armed; one, maybe thirteen or fourteen years old, has a regulation automatic rifle; another—a stringy character with a starter mustache in loose-fitting vest and shorts—holds an unidentifiable (to us at least) piece of weaponry that's almost as tall as him and looks like the hybrid offspring of a shotgun and a blunderbuss. It's easy to forget the casual ease with which guns are handled and displayed in this world.

We park the car and walk through the neighborhood. JB's giving us a guided tour: We see AfroReggae's temporary office; a rehearsal space and its thirteen-year-old caretaker, proud of the responsibility; a kindergarten project full of kids from the ages four to six, each sporting a sky blue AfroReggae T-shirt. We walk down to the front line between Vigário and Lucas. JB thinks it's best if we don't venture too close. We eat lunch at a local joint and, waiting for the food, sit on chairs made of recycled plastic bottles and catch the news on a portable TV. The bulletin is still led by the police killing of Bem-Te-Vi in Rocinha. Everyone is gripped. JB remarks that Bem-Te-Vi was also a homosexual and a hairdresser. Then again, Bem-Te-Vi was the *dono** of the Amigos dos Amigos, a rival faction of Comando Vermelho (and the third in the triumvirate that dominate Rio's favelas), so perhaps the puerile humor of JB's analysis can be taken with a pinch of salt.

Other choices

We meet Luciano and Tota, two ex-*traficantes* who've also recently joined AfroReggae. They've been out of the drug trade about three months.

Luciano is twenty-two, wiry, somewhat diffident but smart and sharp, face hidden by the ubiquitous cap. He worked here in Vigário for eight years, ending up as a "manager." Tota is twenty-four, shaven-headed and softspoken. His last job in the faction was *segurando a fronteira* (literally, "front line secu-

---

* *dono*: the Rio drug trade's top brass. A *dono* will control the traffic in one or more favelas although he will often not live in one of the favelas under his command.

rity"). He's served three years in prison for trafficking. They tell typical stories that conjure typical equations: lack of opportunity plus chance of ready money equals life in the faction. Their attitude is a cocktail of brutal realism and heartfelt aspiration on the rocks.

Ask the pair of them about other choices they might have made and Tota just shrugs. "We have friends who like to steal, go out of the favela to rob banks, shopping malls, and galleries . . . so sure, there are other choices. Sometimes you might get the chance to steal a truck and that might even give you the chance to leave. Things like that give you the opportunity to lead a life that will get you into trouble, but also the chance to get out of it all."

OK. But what about legal options?

Luciano: "There are opportunities for factory work and a lot of people who live in the community and are not involved in drugs, that's what they do. The money's OK and it's not that hard to get a job. You can survive."

Tota: "But you have to wait every month to get your check. In drugs, you get your money on the spot and you're earning about five times what you would in a factory."

JB's analysis of reasons for entering the drug trade runs along similar lines, although he's keen to emphasize that there are all kinds of motivations. As he points out, there are middle-class kids in the trade, too: "Sometimes they want to do it just because they want to do it and that's that."

He is most enlightening, however, when he describes the mentality of the *traficante* and unpicks the psychological trap: "You're fighting the lion, the tiger, and the bird all at the same time, so it [the trafficking] takes you away very fast, takes you over and pulls you in all different directions at once. Once you're into it, you know you might die at the hands of one of the guys who brought you into it. Once you're into it, you're always thinking about the decisions you make and how they affect the others around you. If you make a mistake, you can be killed just like that. So you have to be calculating. All the time, you have to be calculating. Every move you make and every word you say has to be thought out. It's very stressful but you've got to stay cool. That's the mentality. So it's not that you're a bad person to start with but you end up becoming bad because of all the things you have to do. And then you're scarred. That's just how it works."

Tota and Luciano agree that everybody who's been in trafficking for any length of time wants to get out. For Tota, it was his time in prison that convinced him he had to leave. For Luciano, it was the deaths of four good friends in the trade: his cousin, who was killed by the Terceiro Comando, and three others shot by the police. "I saw them die," he says simply, "and I thought I'd be next."

Furthermore, salaries for the *traficantes* have fallen lately as the drug trade in Rio in general and Vigário in particular is squeezed like never before. Citywide this is the result of a combination of factors, from customers being too scared to enter the favelas to the ever-increasing price of protection that has to be paid out to corrupt cops. What's more, the quality of product available in the favelas has fallen just as cocaine has become more readily available in the *asfalto*.

The traffickers in this community face local problems, too. Tota explains it like this: "The invasion [of Vigário by the Terceiro Comando] took place last October at the same time as we had a new boss, so there was a lot of confusion and disruption. Even the addicts in this community started going somewhere else to get their gear."

We wander down to the AfroReggae center we saw on our last visit. It was one of the few two-story buildings in the neighborhood, covered in brightly colored murals, a cathedral of activity and culture amidst the poverty. Now it's just a building site. This is, however, a mark of progress rather than failure, as the organization has just begun the construction of a new facility in its place. When it's finished, it will house a state-of-the-art studio, rehearsal space, and computer rooms, available to the community twenty-four hours a day.

JB gestures to Luciano and Tota. "We live in the jungle," he says. "We were born in the cradle of crime. If AfroReggae hadn't been here? I'll be honest with you: None of us would be alive right now. That's just realistic."

3

First Moves

The *arrastão**

AfroReggae probably owes its existence to a punch-up. One Sunday in October 1992, a huge fistfight between two rival groups of *funk* fans, mostly from the favelas of Vigário Geral and Parada de Lucas, broke out on Arpoador Beach, not far from fashionable Ipanema. The fight caused panic as hundreds of bathers ran for cover amidst the confusion, and some *funkeiros*† took advantage of the chaos to rob the fleeing public. The scenes were broadcast across Brazil on prime-time TV news and, in the context of growing public concern about violence at *baile funk*, the *arrastão* on the beach became the hot topic of debate for candidates contesting the second round of Rio de Janeiro's mayoral election. The direct result of this moral outrage (and, of course, the perceived threat such scenes presented to Rio's tourist industry) was that *funk* parties and the playing of *funk* music in public were outlawed. As decisions go, this can be regarded as one in a long line of

---

* *arrastão*: literally "dragnet." It's a term that has been adopted to describe violence and crime on Rio's beaches, especially coordinated robberies involving teams of youth "trawling" the beach for everything they can lay their hands on.

† *funkeiros*: *funk* fans

knee-jerk reactions on the part of Rio's authorities, addressing the symptoms of a problem rather than its cause. In 2005, for example, the local government banned the sale of postcards showing women's backsides in an attempt, so the story goes, to curb prostitution and sex tourism.

The 1992 *funk* ban, however, caused serious problems for José Junior, then in his early twenties and scratching a living by organizing small *baile*. With advance tickets already sold for his next party, Junior couldn't afford to cancel, so instead he chose to replace the frenetic rhythms of *funk* with the altogether more laid-back sound of reggae. The audience wasn't best pleased by this radical change of tempo, and it was a disaster. Nevertheless, Junior and those working with him were intrigued by the possibility of another reggae party on an altogether bigger scale, partly because Junior's bloody-minded, partly because they still hoped to make some cash, and partly because they were interested in the potential such a party might have to bring together people from different social backgrounds.

As it turned out, "Rasta Reggae Dancing" was a great hit and, according to Junior, the biggest reggae party Rio had ever seen. Buoyed by their success, the gang then came up with an even more unlikely idea: they would produce a newspaper for Rio covering reggae, Afro-Brazilian music, and issues of black interest.

After a good deal of discussion and argument, edition zero of *AfroReggae Noticias*, a four-page newsletter, was launched in January 1993. Throughout that year the number of volunteers producing the paper grew, attracting professional journalists and social activists to its cause. It was during this period that Junior first articulated his desire to offer children growing up in favelas alternatives to criminality: "As a teenager I used to visit various favelas with friends of mine who were picking up drugs. Hanging out with them, I met their friends and I noticed that all the best football players, all the best dancers, and even the kids who drummed on the windows of the bus on their way to the beach . . . they were all from the favela. These talents were gifts and nobody seemed to be taking advantage of them. I thought that if these kids received some sort of support, they might be able to change not only their own lives but also those of the communities themselves."

The massacre

If it was a punch-up that conceived AfroReggae, it was a tragedy that gave birth to the movement. On the night of August 29, 1993, a group of thirty policemen entered Vigário and shot dead twenty-one innocent, unarmed residents. The attack, known as "the Vigário Geral massacre," caused a national and international outcry. Seu Jadir, a survivor of the massacre, describes what happened.

"Nine of us were in the bar. That night, the electricity had cut out in certain parts of the community and I'd fixed it, as I was working for the electricity company at the time. After finishing work, I was just relaxing with a beer. We heard some fireworks going off but because we were all *trabalhadores*,* no one paid attention or got worried by the idea of the police turning up. So we carried on talking in the bar until the police arrived.

"Two policemen came in asking for our papers, which we showed, and a friend told them that we were all workers. The next thing I knew they swore at us, threw an explosive into the bar, and started shooting. They came from everywhere, a whole load from the walkway over the rail tracks, others from

---

* *trabalhadores*: workers. The word is used by both police and favela residents to distinguish between those who work legitimately and the criminals and traffickers, often referred to as *bandidos*.

the side of the favela. They surrounded us. We didn't know they were already getting innocent people and killing them. When they started shooting, we shouted for help but there were people falling to the ground all over the place. I'd been hit and ran into the back of the bar because I knew there was a door there that opened into the yard outside. But while I was trying to open it I was hit by two more bullets and fell. A friend of mine, Ubirajara, got out the door. Coming behind me was another friend who'd been shot, too. He collapsed on top of me and I stayed there until things calmed down. When I finally heard voices I recognized, I called for help and they took me to the hospital.

"Some of the police were wearing balaclavas and others weren't. The first two to arrive weren't. They treated us OK, while the others were shouting and swearing. When the first two came into the bar, the others stayed at the door. After we'd shown them our papers and they went out, the others threw the device in. It exploded and got several people straightaway. It hit a friend of mine, Cláudio, who died. The lights went out when the grenade exploded. It was every man for himself. You couldn't think about saving anyone else.

"I heard the screams of people in agony, but where I was lying, if I'd moved they would have killed me, too. The whole thing lasted between twenty minutes and half an hour. While I was on the floor, I heard more shooting coming from the house of the *crentes*.* Then I heard one of them at the door saying, 'O serviço já está feito.'† I lay there waiting for help. There were nine of us in the bar. Seven died and two of us survived. I was hit by five bullets."

---

* *crentes*: literally, "believers"; in this case, evangelical Christians

† *O serviço já esta feito*: "The job is done."

The killings were provoked by the murder of four police-men the day before by Flávio Negão, then head of drug traf-ficking in Vigário. Just why the police took out their revenge on innocent people remains something of a mystery. Perhaps they were frustrated by their failure to find the traffickers re-sponsible for killing their colleagues or perhaps they were de-liberately targeting civilians. But whatever the reason, there is no doubt that—at least in the eyes of the police—the commu-nity and the drug traffickers from the community had become one and the same thing. Besides the men sharing a quiet drink in the bar, the police also slaughtered passersby and the family of eight evangelical Christians as they sat in their house.

Despite the arrest of all the police believed to have been involved in the attacks, out of some thirty suspects only five have ever been convicted. Although the Vigário Geral massacre stunned Brazil and the world in 1993, it was not even the first such police operation in Rio that year. A few weeks earlier, on July 23, the military police shot dead eight street kids sleeping in the shadow of Candelária Church in the city center.

It was in the aftermath of this appalling state violence that the founders of *AfroReggae Notícias* began to attend commu-nity meetings that took place every Sunday in Vigário and, by June 1994, AfroReggae had established their first Núcleo Co-munitário de Cultura* in the favela. They offered young people workshops in recycling, percussion, and dance, with the clear objective of providing an alternative to drug trafficking and *subemprego*—underemployment. The percussion classes were launched with another *arrastão*, but this one was musical, as a carnival of drummers flooded the streets and alleyways of Vigário with noise and movement.

---

* Núcleo Comunitário de Cultura: Community Nucleus for Culture

Ever since, AfroReggae has continued to launch new community projects with *arrastões*, and they've "reclaimed" for the word a new and positive meaning.

Now

Eleven years on, *AfroReggae Noticias* may have folded but AfroReggae has permanent "nuclei" in three communities—in Vigário, neighboring Lucas, and Cantagalo (a favela in the middle of Rio's affluent Zona Sul [southern zone])—and it's in the process of setting up a fourth in the Complexo do Alemão. AfroReggae is fronted by their main band, who've just released their second major label album, *Nenhum Motivo Explica a Guerra* (*There Is No Motive for War*). But beneath the main band there are twelve subgroups that include dance, theatre, and circus troupes; a samba school; and a reggae band. AfroReggae organizes more than sixty projects in numerous communities, touching thousands. One of their most successful and high-profile projects is called *Connexões Urbanas*—Urban Connections—which they produce in conjunction with the city government. This is a series of free concerts given in favelas that, importantly, match the production quality of similar events in the rich neighborhoods. The AfroReggae band performs at every one but they are usually joined onstage by local stars. Since 2001, more than forty such concerts have taken place, featuring everyone from the Brazilian legend, founder of the "Tropicália" movement, and current minister of culture, Gilberto Gil, to top *funk* DJ Marlboro and multiplatinum São Paulo hip-hop crew Racionais MCs.

Every AfroReggae nucleus has a different approach that has been designed over time and tailored to the needs of the parent community. Whereas the organization's presence in Vigário, for example, is primarily cultural, with the emphasis on music, theatre, and dance, in Lucas they have a computer and technology center, bringing state-of-the-art equipment and training to the favela. Cantagalo, on the other hand, part of a complex of three favelas high on the hillsides above Copacabana and Ipanema, is where the circus project is based.

The target audience for AfroReggae's work is not limited to these poor communities alone. In 2004, they launched a project to bring culture to the military police battalions of Minas Gerais, a neighboring state. The intention has been to blitz them with what AfroReggae calls "cultural invasions," offering workshops in percussion, dance, streetball, graffiti, and theatre for one week each month over a four-month period. The percussion group resulting from these "invasions" has been so successful that it has been featured twice on one of Brazil's most watched television shows, the Sunday afternoon *Faustão* show, broadcast on the Globo network.

Since 1997, AfroReggae has received funding grants from the Ford Foundation as part of its human-rights initiative. Denise Doura, program officer for the Foundation in Rio, has long recognized AfroReggae's capacity to make a little money go a long way, and here she tries to assess the success of their projects and give a snapshot of the context in which they work.

"One of the main reasons for the success of AfroReggae is that they do things from the heart. They genuinely have an interest, talking to people and making sure that they [Afro-Reggae] understand the issues. I have been following them closely for the last five years and sometimes I feel their reaction to some situations is initially very instinctive. Then they start elaborating what they've done, they understand their own behavior, and create a methodology.

"The killing of young people is one of the main human-rights problems in Brazil; both in terms of impunity and the public acceptance that allows police or others to carry out these killings. Unfortunately, they are so common now that people just accept them without being made to feel in any way uncomfortable. This is a key problem for Brazilian society as a whole. When you can live with arbitrary executions without any reaction, that's a horrible situation. And of course, the killings target young people who have no access to education. Some of the favelas in Rio only have an elementary school. For example, fifty thousand people live in Cidade de Deus—City of God—but there's no secondary school.

"Young people don't have any professional training and can't find jobs, so what do they do? They can't work, so how can they survive? On the one hand you have this lack of opportunity, on the other the possibilities of the city's drug trade. And the state and wider society do nothing about this dilemma. Instead, the only solution that's been tried is to kill these youth as soon as they've crossed the line between missing school and committing crime. And that's a very fine line.

"The traditional human-rights organizations don't work in this situation. They have a lot of other things to do, and they simply don't have access to these communities. When I started working for the Ford Foundation, one of the first things I noticed was that traditional NGOs were not present in this world. But AfroReggae was.

"When you consider the context—the problems of police and government, the attitudes of the people in Zona Sul and the Carioca middle class—I do think that AfroReggae might be the solution for the situation in Rio. If you see the right thing to do, you just have to do it. That's what AfroReggae does and that's why they're so effective and so important."

4

Rival Factions

In many respects, AfroReggae bears little resemblance to any typical NGO. If anything, it seems to have more in common with the Rio de Janeiro drug factions. Walk through Vigário Geral and you'll spot two groups communicating by short-wave radio and giving every appearance of commanding the narrow streets. One is a sullen bunch with seemingly nothing to do but roll one joint after the next, the other is full of purpose and activity, carrying a drum here, rushing to a meeting there. One group will be clutching state-of-the-art firearms, the other wearing loud AfroReggae T-shirts.

What's more, just as in the factions, membership in Afro-Reggae requires adhering to a disciplined lifestyle. Members are, for example, forbidden to drink or smoke, let alone use drugs. Like the factions, they have a rigid and recognizable hierarchy that can be climbed by a committed individual. These similarities are, of course, all part of José Junior's plan. Junior is AfroReggae's founder and executive coordinator or, to use the language of the factions, its *dono*.

If AfroReggae is not your typical NGO, then Junior is certainly not your typical NGO boss. Junior is a charismatic storyteller, a laid-back disciplinarian, a humble man of irrepressible certainty, and an unashamed capitalist entrepreneur with a big, big heart. He is also all restless energy and endless multitasking. A conversation with Junior will often be conducted while he has one ear pressed to his radio, the other to his mobile phone, and his eyes fixed to the screen of his laptop, dealing with a pressing e-mail.

The first time we meet Junior in Rio, however, it is a public holiday (the Day of the Dead) and the atmosphere in his comfortable flat in Glória in downtown Rio is a little less frenetic than usual. His wife is chatting to his mother in the kitchen and his daughters dart in and out. JB is there, too, a hefty but silent presence watching from the corner.

Junior lounges in an armchair in shorts, flip-flops, and an AfroReggae T-shirt. How old is he? Late thirties, but he could easily pass for younger. He has recognizably *nordestino** features and his chunky earrings make him look more than a little like a pirate. Opposite him a huge wall-hanging of Ganesh, the Hindu god of success, takes up an entire side of the room. Junior became fascinated by Hinduism in his early twenties and AfroReggae's philosophy is driven by a belief in Shiva, the god of transformation: destroyer and restorer, both ascetic and sensual, the wrathful avenger and the kindly herdsman of souls.

Junior is already talking as we sit down. The head of the Comando Vermelho in Vigário has asked for his help. He wants to get out of trafficking, and Junior describes how this might happen: "This guy will not be joining AfroReggae. He's illiterate and he needs some training. Hopefully, he'll start a business

---

* *nordestino*: northeastern. This word refers not only to origin, but often also to appearance, a mixture of European, African, and indigenous heritage typical of the region.

outside Rio. I'll bankroll this. Can you guess what he wants to do? Raise pigs and chickens. Originally he's from the state interior and he came to Rio as a child, so he misses that time in his life.

"Do I think he'll stay out of traffic forever? I don't know, but I'm trying. In all my twelve years with AfroReggae there's never been a trafficker who's come to me for as much help as this guy. This is the work we've always done: taking people out of the traffic and stopping people getting into it has always been our combined priority. Up until 1996, one of our singers, LG, was a manager, a high-ranking position. Now he stands as one of the best examples of our success."

At this point, JB gets up and goes to the kitchen. He returns a moment later with glasses, ice, and cans of Red Bull for everyone. Red Bull is one of AfroReggae's sponsors. Junior gestures to JB and embarks on a story that encapsulates the intuitive and subversive style of AfroReggae's work.

"JB?" Junior begins. "He was in the *cúpula*** of trafficking. From his generation, only JB and one other guy have survived. It's impossible to say how many more there were who are now dead. And JB is so important to AfroReggae; not just because he is an astonishing conflict mediator but also because he's someone with knowledge and wisdom that have never been systematically recorded in any way.

"I'll give you an example: Last Friday I sent JB to a *baile funk* in Complexo do Alemão. He took three police officers from our project in Minas Gerais and the Brazilian director of a multinational bank who was visiting from São Paulo. It was important for them to see a *baile* firsthand and good to mix police with the director of a multinational. They were having

---

* *cúpula*: the top level

a great time: The local girls were dancing away with the cops, things like that. Unfortunately, an extremely unusual thing happened. At three thirty in the morning, the police entered the favela.

"That same night on the other side of Rio, the police had just killed Bem-Te-Vi, the head of traffic in Rocinha [Amigos dos Amigos territory]. So what happens? The people who might attack Rocinha come from Alemão, so the cops—the BOPE*— come into the favela in order to suffocate any action, to prevent Comando Vermelho taking advantage of the situation and invading Rocinha.

"But the police came up to the party shooting like crazy. Even JB says he's never heard the police shooting so much in his life. Why? Firstly, to stamp out any attempt by the traffickers to attack Rocinha. Secondly, because the police know that *baile funk* in favelas are put on by the factions.

"Now, every time I ask JB to take someone to the favela I tell him that their lives are in his hands. The cops may have just been shooting in the air but still, ten people were hit. JB is so loyal that he took the three cops and the banker by the hand, used his body as a shield, and found a safe escape route out of all the confusion. He called me at dawn.

"JB has a disposition derived from his experience, which should be looked at closely. It is what I call the positive effects of *o tráfico*: hierarchy and discipline. JB has profound notions of both these things and he learned them in the faction. When he was working in trafficking, he says he was told by his boss that, whatever needed doing, he had to get the job done and always keep his eyes on the prize.

---

* BOPE: Batalhão de Operações Especiais, an elite miltary police unit specifically trained in favela operations

"The day after this incident at the *baile*, the director of the bank called me and said that he now had a new blood brother—JB. So we have two completely different realities put side by side that now have mutual respect. The banker phoned me again yesterday to discuss some of the projects that they're supporting, and he kept asking me how JB was doing. There's an AfroReggae show in São Paulo next week and he's asked me to make sure JB comes, too.

"I'm telling you about this for the following reason: even though the traffic is criminal, a 'bad thing,' so to speak, it has some extremely positive aspects; like loyalty, discipline, and hierarchy. These days, I am JB's boss. When I told him yesterday that he would be looking after *you*, I told him each of your backgrounds and I said to him, 'JB, I trust these guys and you can open everything to them. Anything that happens to them is your responsibility and their lives are in your hands.'

"Look at the way JB stands. Even when he's silent, he stands next to you in a way that physically protects you. So JB is security, a conflict mediator, a PR guy and, above all, a guy who has a huge knowledge of the way things work: He is all of these things in one character."

Junior's story hints at three key aspects of AfroReggae's methodology. There is an area of Vigário that, somewhat ironically, has the same name as the federal capital: Brasília. It was here that Afro Lata, one of AfroReggae's subgroups, was founded by boys aged between ten and fifteen. They were excited by the percussion of another subgroup, Makala, but since AfroReggae had no spare drums and no money to buy them, they had to make do with whatever they had. So they chopped up old broomsticks and turned barrels, plastic tubs, and buckets into musical instruments. They are now one of the organization's most successful projects. For AfroReggae, therefore, an ex-trafficker is a potential source of knowledge as surely as a discarded oil drum is a potential source of rhythm.

In an increasingly divided city where favelas are excluded communities considered out of bounds by citizens from the *asfalto*, AfroReggae determinedly crosses boundaries. For the groups this frequently means taking their performances (and thus, by extension, favela culture) out of the communities and to the world beyond; but, for the organization, it also means introducing that world to some of the harsher realities of the situation in which they work. When Junior arranges for a high-powered banker from São Paulo to visit a *baile* in Complexo do Alemão, therefore, he is introducing a potential partner to both the positive (in the party itself) and the negative (in the action of the police, albeit unexpected) manifestations of favela life.

This second point leads finally to the key role played by Junior himself. His is a delicate position indeed as he negotiates with senior figures in the traffic, the media, business, police, and politics. He carries it off through force of personality, the proven success of AfroReggae's work, and the quality of the relationships he's developed: one such is undoubtedly with JB, another may yet be with the banker from São Paulo.

5

JB Tells His Story

The dream

"I dream that I'm sitting on Avenida Brasil just in front of the entrance to Parada de Lucas. I've hurt my foot. I'm sitting there, no shoes on, with a pistol in my lap. There's a football match going on in Nova Holanda—*futebol da paz*—a 'peace' game between Vigário Geral and Lucas. It's raining and I'm tired. I want to go to the match but I'm stuck there for some reason, completely exhausted. Some kid wearing a baseball cap and carrying a walkie-talkie emerges from Lucas. I can see two pistols under his shirt. He walks past, looks back, catches my eye, and starts grilling me: '*Que tu está fazendo aí?*'—'What are you doing?'

"I tell him that the traffickers from Lucas know I'm there. I tell him that they're playing football in Nova Holanda and I can't because of my bad foot. I know that the two factions are at war but this is *futebol da paz*, and the boss of Lucas knows who I am and that I'm here. This kid shouldn't be starting an argument with me.

"I stand up, face him, and say, 'Let's go to Lucas then.'

"We walk into the favela and I sit down at a bar. I begin to eat a plate of rice and beans which I cover with *farinha*.* There are some traffickers from Lucas surrounding me but they can't do anything because of the *futebol da paz*. While I'm eating, the Lucas team gets back—they've lost. They're really pissed off and when they get there the kid starts telling them, 'Look here's JB *cheio de marra*!'—acting like he's the man. The *dono* says that he knows me and it's cool. I look at the door and the traffickers from Vigário are coming in. Everyone's got guns.

"I wake up in a sweat. I dream about these things every day. Sometimes I'm traveling around Brazil with Junior and I dream about deaths I witnessed in the favelas when I was a *traficante*."

Family and roots

"My father and mother brought me up well. But the sheer energy of the favela made me want to live another way. By the time I was twelve, I wanted to be a drug trafficker, a *bandido*. The traffickers used to give us money—if you wanted to buy a kite or something, you'd just have to ask them. I thought it was the best thing in the world.

"I was born in the favela of Vigário. My mother was born and raised there, too. My father is a sailor from Maranhão and, when I was twelve, we all went to live outside in the *asfalto*. My dad was in the navy and he had enough money to send us to a private school. My brothers and sisters kept on at school but I was never into studying, so I spent my days hanging out in Vigário. I only went home to sleep. My brothers and sisters always studied and went to church. When I was ten or eleven I went to church but, even then, I preferred spending my time in the favela. All my brothers and sisters devoted themselves to

---

* *farinha*: a popular Brazilian condiment made with coarse manioc flour

study. Not me. They're all married and live with their families in Rio. I don't see them much."

Cuco

"Cuco and I were brought up together, friends from the *baile funk* days. He was the head of the *galera** from Vigário. In 1993, I stopped going to the *baile* and got a job. Like the majority of my friends from the *funk* days, Cuco got involved in the drug business. When the massacre took place, he was already working as a trafficker. I used to go and talk to people for him and do jobs for him outside the favela, but only ever as a friend. I didn't get involved myself until a couple of years later."

The van

"In 1994, I bought a Volkswagen van—a combi—for freight work. I used to transport people and goods all over the place. I loved that van. While I was working away quietly, my friend Cuco was earning lots and lots of money.

"At around the same time Cuco bought a brand-new combi that he gave to his uncle who looked after all his legitimate business interests. But this uncle could hardly drive and he kept denting the van. One day Cuco asked me to give him a lift to a hotel where he was meeting a girl. I dropped him off and left the van with his uncle. Cuco spent the night there. Although he was rich, the police weren't looking for him then. At the time, he was one of a group of traffickers who lived and worked inside Vigário but earned most of their money from *bocas*† they ran in other favelas.

---

* *galera*: group. In the context of *funk*, *galera* is used to refer to a group from a specific neighborhood.

† *boca*: short for *boca de fumo*. Literally "mouth of smoke." The factions' sales outlets where the traffickers generally hang out.

"The next day I went to pick him up. He was with the girl and asked me to take them to the shopping mall to buy clothes. When we got there, he pulled 3,000 Reais* out of his pocket. This wasn't much money for him. He was earning thousands every day. He was in charge of various favelas, and sales ten years ago were three times what they are today. He bought lots of designer clothes for himself: the best trainers, shorts, and jeans. But he also bought clothes for his girlfriend and me, too. Me? I was *sofredor*,† sweating in my combi for a tiny salary. Honest sweat, honest work. I could never have got what he bought for me. I'd have needed to save for months.

"At this point in time I'd never been involved in crime: never done a robbery, nothing. I wouldn't have hurt a fly. He said, 'Choose what you want. Help yourself.'

"I picked some clothes. He paid. After that he gave me 500 Reais. I was speechless. You might think I got involved with him because I thought I needed that stuff. In reality I didn't. But I never saw him as a *traficante*. He might have been the boss of his gang but I didn't see him like that. I only saw him as my friend, a guy that I grew up with. He was someone I wound up, joked around with, and insulted. His *soldados* couldn't believe the way I talked to him.

"At the beginning I told Cuco that he should get out of it, that he'd die. But when someone's got all that power, they don't care. I used to tell him, '*sai dessa parada*'—leave this game—before you die like all the others. But the atmosphere in Vigário was completely intoxicating. People there were dripping money and gold. The *boca* was famous and sales were good, so it was very unlikely that anyone would think about leaving crime back then.

---

* At the time, approximately $3,000

† *sofredor*: a sufferer

"One day he asked me for a favor. Because I had a clean license, he asked me to look after the combi that his uncle was smashing to bits. I happily accepted because he was my friend and I gave my van to my cousin who was unemployed. The same night that he asked me to look after his combi, a kid came over to my house saying that Cuco needed me in Vigário. I got out of bed and, when I reached him, he asked if I could take him to the hotel again. And that's how it started. He gave me 500 Reais a week. It was just to look after the van, hang out, and drive him around."

The kidnap

"Now I'm going to try and explain how I got really deep into o tráfico.

"At the beginning of 1996, there was a serious internal dispute between the various traffickers based in Vigário. Because of this, Cuco, along with a very prominent member of the Comando Vermelho, went to live in the favela of Borel in Tijuca. I was already involved with Cuco through driving but had still never taken part in anything explicitly criminal. I'd never transported drugs or guns.

"However, as Cuco's driver, I automatically went along, too. So, while one group of traficantes stayed in Vigário, we all went to Borel. I only went there to work, though, and at night I still used to come home to my family in Vigário. But at this point things began to move fast. The gerente geral* of Borel was arrested and Cuco took over while he was in prison. At the same time, the dispute with the guys in Vigário was getting out of hand. They began by threatening our families and then, one night, mounted a failed plan to kill me. Because of all this I decided to move permanently to Borel.

---

* gerente geral: general manager, senior rank in o tráfico

"Around then I was arrested for the first time. In fact, I was kidnapped. The police stopped me and Cuco in the combi when we were leaving Borel. This was the first time that we'd ever been picked up by them, and they asked for money to let us go. Cuco stayed behind and I was dispatched to come up with the ransom. I went to Borel, spoke to people, and we got a load of money together: a million Reais. Along with this we threw in several kilos of gold, forty pistols, and twelve machine guns. This was the ransom that we paid and it all came from stocks we'd built up in Borel. Me and a friend from the *boca* were the ones who dealt with the police. I drove to the meeting point in the combi and we lost that, too. This was the very first time that I'd driven any weapons in the van and here I was delivering them to the cops.

"From that moment on I began to take part directly. We didn't go down to the *asfalto* anymore and I began to carry a gun. I had my own AR-15. We didn't like pistols. Those of us working in security preferred to carry machine guns or rifles. We gave the handguns to the kids who were working as look-outs."

The trafficking life

"Three or four years in this life feels like an eternity. You don't sleep; you have nightmares all the time. You see ten people being murdered all at once. You might be eating your lunch and just next to you someone is *picoteando*—quartering—a body. Kids are dying here, women there. People are executed for making mistakes. People are betraying each other. You're being shot at by the police. Your friends are getting killed at your side.

"You're living in hell and the devil talks to you. You read the Bible to see if you can relax, go to evangelical church, ask people to pray for you. You're hoping something will change but it doesn't. You get used to living in a bloodbath. You smoke loads of *maconha** to try and relax and end up going for two or three days without sleeping. You hide in the forest because the police are looking for you.

"I might be sitting joking with a friend one minute and have to shoot him the next because the guy in charge of the *boca* has ordered me to kill him. And I've got to kill him coldly. At the same time you have to keep a close watch on those around you to make sure they're not jealous, that so-and-so hasn't got a beef with you, that he isn't plotting to kill you, too. And you have to be mates, shake each other by the hand, and stick together until death. You give your life for the boss because he is the boss of your life, the boss of everyone's life in the communities he's running.

"I learned from the older traffickers that you can do many brave things . . . invade and take over enemy favelas, fight wars, or defend your territory against the police. . . . You can do all these things, but if you make a mistake or mess up even once, you'll be eliminated.

"With Cuco I was safe. We looked out for each other. At the same time, in the middle of it all, I didn't really ever know where I was. I consider myself a war veteran. You will never know what it's like to be waiting in a favela, holding a machine gun, knowing that anything can happen at any time in any way. That's what crime is."

Getting out

"In 1999, out of some seventy guys I started out with, only thirty of us were alive and not in prison. I wanted out because I'd already lived a normal life and desperately needed to get back to it. I was scared, though. I couldn't walk in the streets.

---

* *maconha*: marijuana

I was terrified that an enemy or the police would kill me. Back then, Cuco was still alive, too. He was arrested twice more but never with me. And each time he paid the police off. In truth, he was kidnapped, not arrested. It was Cuco who helped me begin to get out, because he was my friend. He asked me to start organizing *funk* events in the community. We moved on to Morro da Formiga, which we had taken over from the Terceiro Comando. That became Cuco's base and we passed Borel on to others. So I started putting on parties. These were paid for with trafficking money. Cuco asked me to do this and moved me away from working as a soldier.

"By now AfroReggae had been working in Vigário for a while. We all knew about them and admired what they did because we knew they were a group of kids from Vigário who'd been changing the favela. We'd watched their work over the years and heard what was happening from our relatives. They began to travel abroad and we saw Anderson* and the others on TV.

"In 2000, Junior had a problem there and a friend of mine named Celso came looking for me. He knew me from a job I'd done with the rapper MV Bill. At the time I only knew Junior by name, I'd never met him. I hadn't been to Vigário for ages, even though the old group of *traficantes* had left and we got on OK with the new bunch. But now someone had threatened Junior and Cuco asked me to find out what the problem was. It was the first time I'd been there for years.

"In the end it was no more than a misunderstanding that was easily resolved. It changed my life, though, because I sat down with Junior. We made friends and he asked me to come and work for him. At the beginning I didn't want to; I was

---

* Anderson is one of the vocalists in AfroReggae's main band.

scared of being outside the favela. I still hadn't gotten out of that way of thinking and the prospect of life on the *asfalto* frightened me. This mind-set is something that I'll never be able to completely leave behind. Then Junior told me his plans for Conexões Urbanas. When he told me, I thought he was joking: No one was going to get Gilberto Gil and Caetano Veloso to perform in the favela. I told him to get serious—there was no way I'd sit down with the bosses and tell them that, because they'd laugh in my face. I didn't know how big AfroReggae was.

"The first event was in the Complexo do Alemão, co-organized with the Prefeitura, Viva Rio,* and so on. The area where it was held used to be a garbage dump but because of the show they cleared it up permanently. For the next Urban Connections, I asked if we could do it in Formiga. It was cool. There were no drugs or guns and it became our passport to other events. By 2002, I'd been working with AfroReggae for two years."

The second kidnap

"In 2002, one day before an Urban Connections show in a place called Vila Kennedy, we were checking the sound out. It was about four in the afternoon and I was hanging around with the production team when the police appeared. A friend saw them coming but I wasn't worried. I'd been involved in lots of these events and nothing had ever happened. Then this cop pointed his machine gun at me and said, 'JB! *Perdeu!*'—the game's up. *Perdeu* [literally: it's lost] is the word thieves use when they're about to rob someone and police use when they catch a crook. Three policemen in uniform sat down with me in the car. Everyone was watching. No one understood what

---

* Prefeitura: municipal government (literally: prefecture); Viva Rio: one of the largest and best-known Rio NGOs

was going on. Inside the car there was a guy in normal clothes: an X-9.* He spoke to me: 'Well, JB, didn't I say that I'd get you one day?' I'd never seen him before in my life.

"We drove off. I was sitting in the back between two of the cops. We drove to Avenida Brasil and then Vila Aliança, a community that belongs to the Amigos dos Amigos faction and is the base of one of its leaders. They took me to a police outpost, which was a real mess. There was blood on the walls and it must have been somewhere they took people to extort money. It was a community policing post in the middle of the favela. All the time this guy in plainclothes kept telling me that he'd said he'd get me, and he kept asking about Cuco and other Comando Vermelho leaders. But what he really wanted was money and he kept trying to scare me. They kept repeating, 'Do you know where you are?' And they told me that if no one came up with some money, they'd hand me over to the enemies.

"I was desperate because I knew what was in the cards. If they handed me over, I'd be tortured, quartered, or burned—maybe all three. I told them I worked for AfroReggae, but they said they didn't know what it was.

"In the meantime, Junior had been informed what was happening and started to mobilize everyone he could: Viva Rio, the UN, everyone. The state governor was Garotinho, and his secretary called the chief of police. In the post where the cops had me there was a Maria Zero† and it crackled: 'Sargento X? Sargento X? Please could you confirm whether Jorge Luis Passos Mendes is in your company. I repeat, where is the man that you picked up in Vila Kennedy?' The chief of police said he was sending a squad car over.

---

* X-9: favela slang for a police informant
† Maria Zero: police frequency radio

"The cops who'd picked me up started arguing with each other, and the X-9 who'd threatened me started shouting at them, gesticulating, saying, 'That's him! That's JB!'

"I was taken to the local police station. When we got there, the civil police were all looking at me. I thought I'd had it. The senior officer had a piece of paper in his hand and I was shaking.

"He asked who I was and, even though I didn't know what I should say, I confirmed my name. He looked at me and said, 'You see these three policemen? Do you want to press charges against them for kidnapping?' I froze. He continued: 'I don't know who you are and I don't know what AfroReggae is. I just know that you've managed to get the governor involved in this; that the governor phoned the public security secretary who phoned the chief of police who phoned me.'

"I could have had those police behind me arrested. But, knowing what I know, I just said, 'Sir, these police arrested me because they thought I'd committed a crime. They searched me and nothing else happened.'"

The future

"Since I joined AfroReggae, Junior's always tried to show me things from other worlds: other information, other types of music, computers, and so on. But you can't get away from the world that you lived in, the perverse things that you saw and did. Even those things that you enjoyed haunt you. All this has sunk into your unconscious and you can't escape it.

"However, to do my work for AfroReggae, I *need* to have this side to me. In a way the work in itself is a cure and my knowledge is the instrument that I use to orient the whole institution. When everyone from AfroReggae leaves the favela and goes home, I sit and talk to the *traficantes* because there are people there who trust me and tell me things that they wouldn't even tell the guy sitting next to them. I have to keep doing this, having conversations and swapping ideas. If I stopped, they'd look at me differently and I wouldn't be able to come back with the same degree of access that I have now. I'd lose credibility.

"Children aren't born criminals. The boy who picks up a gun when he's three or four just wants to play. He doesn't know what the gun means. As he grows up he sees what's around him and, even more, he sees what is denied him. I think that for things to get better in this country, we Brazilians have to look to ourselves first, to our reality. We mustn't look outside for results. We must try to change things from within.

"I think that not even the president can resolve things, principally because of the people who surround him. In order to begin to tackle this mess, we need to start by working in the state schools. We need good people to work as teachers and more opportunities for these excluded areas. The fundamental thing is opportunity. When a kid finds out that things are closed off to him, things get worse. I think that the future requires that we think ten years ahead and start working now on things that will work for kids in the communities. We need culture and education for them and we need to plan for the result ten years from now. Because, at the moment, there is no way that we can make things better. This is my vision.

"In the work of AfroReggae, we're aware that we're doing our bit. When we manage to get two or three guys out of trafficking, we're doing our bit. You get them out and then you start to see results. It's not like some projects that abandon youth. If that happens, the expectations of the youth are shattered—that's the worst thing that can happen.

"The words 'favela' and '*comunidade*' are very strong,

beautiful words. I could do many things but I'm not going to change my life right now, because these are my roots and this is my reality. I'm used to living this way. I think that all of us working in AfroReggae realize that we have an immense amount of work left to do. We do it because we like it, because we want to, and because there's a need for it. I've lost all my childhood friends. If they'd had the opportunity to change their lives in the way I did, I'm certain that they would have done so. Today I talk to these kids working as *traficantes*, and I know they want to get out. But they can't, because there are no opportunities for them to do so. And that's why I'm here."

6

The Political Moment

The corruption scandal that brought the work of Brazil's federal government to a grinding halt in 2005 was all-consuming. Allegations, counterallegations, commissions of inquiry, firings, and speculation blocked the papers and jammed the television news. Some ministers and top aides avoided the noose while others, such as President Lula's prominent former right-hand man, José Dirceu, were not so lucky. Skeletons, like that of Celso Daniel, the PT* mayor who was gunned down outside a São Paulo restaurant in 2002, were hauled out of the closet and dusted down for renewed inspection. Nothing was beyond question. Old certainties crumbled without any new ones to take their place. But, individual Brazilians had no choice but to get on with their lives against a seamy backdrop of political and moral decline.

After twenty years of trying, Luiz Inácio Lula da Silva, leader of the PT, had swept to power in January 2003 on a tide of optimism and goodwill. Less than three years later, his administration was imploding. Even the most politically cynical

---

* PT: Partido dos Trabalhadores, The Workers' Party

Brazilian (of which there are a fair few) would have struggled to predict the scale of the fall.

The scandal was, in fact, several scandals in one—a hugely complicated web of corruption that we're not going to attempt to unpick here. But at its heart were payments made by the government to federal congressmen for their support (as the PT were a minority in Congress). It wasn't just the scale of the corruption, however, that was so shocking. It was also that it implicated (albeit indirectly) Lula, the honest man of the people, the benchmark of political integrity.

Despite this, many of the millions who supported Lula merely shrugged and accepted it as yet another chapter of disappointment in the turbulent story of Brazilian central government. However, while his core support, especially the poor, voted for him again in 2006, the middle-class electorate was a lot more skeptical. And for those who devoted their lives to building the PT across the country for more than twenty years, it was a catastrophe.

The opponent

Waiting for a delayed Varig flight one morning at Rio de Janeiro's international airport in late 2005, we sit behind someone who seems to know an awful lot. The man is a professional footballer working in Europe, who knows so much about everything that he talks to the couple next to him confidently and nonstop for the better part of an hour. Topics covered include traffic (the type with cars), weather, cooking, exchange rates, football, and politics. When he begins to discuss the PT, his voice strains with unconcealed venom.

"We always knew they were woolly, incompetent assholes—and now we know they're crooks as well. They pretended they were better than everyone else, now look at them! Look at what they've done!

"At least the other guys don't pretend they're going to save us all. And we know they steal. Everyone steals." What comes next is all too predictable, the weary mantra that has been used to justify corruption in Brazil for decades. "But at least they do something. Maluf in São Paulo, for instance. He might have been a crook, but look at all he did for the city. I believe in the saying '*Rouba mas faz*.'"

Rouba mas faz: he steals but he gets things done. The former mayor of São Paulo, together with his son, is at that moment in police custody. They stand accused of money laundering, corruption, and *formação de quadrilha*—forming a criminal gang. They are also believed to have intimidated witnesses who are due to testify before federal investigators gathering information about some $161 million, allegedly siphoned off from municipal funds and transferred to U.S. bank accounts.

The mud has stuck. For many conservative Brazilians and loyal supporters of politicians such as Maluf and others like him (who might embezzle public money but are considered efficient), the federal government corruption scandal has confirmed what they have often asserted: The PT is not just a bunch of dangerous left-wingers but, underneath it all, they're the same as the rest. They steal. In short, as the man at the airport says: "*Roubam, mas fazem porra nenhuma!*" They steal but they do fuck-all!

Civil society

Maybe it's a trick of the light, but when asked about the implications of the political crisis, Denise Doura from the Brazilian office of the Ford Foundation's eyes appear to fill. She shakes her head: "I think it's going to take some time for us to recover, because we've been enormously let down by a number of people. I was in my twenties when democratization took place, so I'm part of the generation that was involved in rebuilding the country and writing the constitution. I think that we've achieved a lot in twenty-five years: coming from a military dictatorship to a country where we have free elections and well-organized institutions. However, this is a very hard, difficult lesson for our generation."

Nevertheless, Denise also stresses the potential value of this lesson. If it hadn't happened, she says, Brazil would be in the hands of a populist, patriarchal government that wouldn't actually have implemented the changes the country requires. "We need more. I think that people are slowly realizing that we need to pay more attention to what is going on in society as a whole, not just in the government and the public sphere. We're starting to realize that perhaps NGOs will have to last more than ten or fifteen years.

"Now it's like a hangover the day after the party. People living and working in Brasília are very depressed. People in Congress say that it no longer makes any sense to talk to this or that parliamentarian because they know all they'll hear is lies. People don't trust the institutions anymore and I think that this distrust will last a while. But overall I don't think it's too bad, because I'd like to see a more civic life in Brazil, a life that isn't so attached to government.

"Of course, it will take a long time to get over the crisis but when you talk to people, you see that they're already thinking about the future. They may not even be bothered about the elections next year. Instead, they're thinking, 'Let's do something else.' In ten years it might mean that we'll have a more mature society."

Someone else with a ten-year vision? Denise almost sounds like JB.

Civil society in Brazil has always played a major part in developing public policy and legislation. To an extent, this is based on the commonly held assumption that government will eventually resolve problems and that, therefore, the role of civil society is to provide government with problem-solving proposals. As a result, most social movements have traditionally looked to their elected representatives to eventually, they hope, change the status quo. But perhaps the profound disappointment in the Lula government (even though it's far from being the only crisis-hit administration since the return to democracy) may finally change the notion that the Brazilian state has the will, let alone the capacity, to resolve all of society's ills. In Denise's eyes, anyway, governments are as much part of the problem as the solution and, in the meantime, there are plenty of other things to be getting on with.

"And this is what AfroReggae does," Denise says, suddenly enthused. "It knows that governments will come and go but that we'll all still be here. So it's worth trying to do something that can survive over time. Sure, the state must develop some sort of infrastructure in the places where we work and promote public policies that target the groups we're working with, but we must also recognize that this is neither the solution to the problem, nor an end in itself."

Disarmament

On October 23, 2005, Brazil held a national referendum proposing a ban on commercial arms sales to civilians. The referendum was one element of the Disarmament Statute, a law passed in December 2003 that essentially criminalized carrying guns for anyone other than the armed forces, the police, and other public and private security forces. Initial opinion polls suggested that the Brazilian population was largely in favor of the sales ban. The pro-disarmament lobby, backed by prominent NGOs such as Viva Rio and the São Paulo–based Sou da Paz, promoted a "Yes" campaign based, obviously enough, on the idea that fewer firearms in circulation would reduce overall violence. Indeed, the campaign had a decent precedent in São Paulo where gun control—seizures of illegal weapons and a reduction in the number of licenses issued—was a vital factor in the marked reduction in homicide rates since 1997.

In response to the early opinion polls, however, an efficient and extremely well-financed gun lobby mobilized to defend the right to buy arms. And their central argument tapped straight into Brazilians' very darkest fears: Who will look after you if all the guns belong to criminals and criminals alone? Who will protect the average citizen if the state won't?

Questions like these exploited the deep-seated public terror of violent crime—the same terror that has been used to justify repressive, violent policing for decades. It was a tactic that went directly to the core of the most sensitive and conservative areas of the national psyche. And it worked.

In Rio, the day before the vote, a pro-disarmament procession through the rich Zona Sul neighborhood was booed and jeered by residents who rushed from their apartment buildings to taunt the campaigners. The next day, every one of Brazil's twenty-six states delivered a resounding "No" vote.

And yet the collapse of public support for disarmament cannot be blamed on fear alone. It is probable that, for some voters, the referendum actually represented a vote of no confidence in the Lula government. Commentators have contrasted the celebrity-driven haziness of the "Yes" campaign with the clinical efficiency of the "No" lobby, but there is also no doubt that the referendum forced Brazilians through the usual electoral motions and therefore into the usual electoral mind-set. As when electing political representatives, the vote was mandatory—citizens having to justify absence or face a fine. As when electing political representatives, hour upon hour of prime-time television was dedicated to "Yes" or "No" propaganda. Then, Lula and other prominent members of his party publicly aligned themselves with the "Yes" campaign. Even though Brazilians were not actually electing anyone, who could blame those who felt as if that was exactly what they were doing? And it seems that many of them chose to vote against Lula.

Luiz Eduardo Soares, formerly both Rio state secretary and national secretary for public security (and author of the public security proposal that was a highly regarded element of the PT's 2002 election manifesto) believes the federal government's proximity to the "Yes" campaign was the kiss of death for the movement. According to Luiz Eduardo, the political crisis and the disorientation that it produced in PT supporters were fundamental in undermining the campaign. He states his hypothesis thus: "I talked to many people, especially students, who would naturally vote 'Yes' and naturally be on the left side of the political spectrum. But the fact that the PT is so demoralized had an incredible impact on the situation, producing a wide fragmentation of opinion."

Luiz Eduardo explains that Brazilians have only really understood the importance of the PT now that it has collapsed and can no longer be considered a useful model with which to identify. "The process of formation of political ideas is one of social and cultural identification. Of course there is also reasoning, argument, and reflection, but the most significant process is one of identification. In the past, when youngsters didn't know what to think about an issue, they'd look to Lula to find out what he was thinking and, depending on his position, would then define their own standpoint. But now? I've been with students who say the most incredible things, mixing progressive thought with reactionary ideas in complete confusion. Because this point of reference, this axis, is not there anymore. Of course it will come back together at some point, but not before next year's election. It will take years and years to rebuild."

The collapse of the credibility of the PT government and the victory of the conservative "No" vote in the disarmament referendum seemed to represent the end of a hopeful moment in Brazilian politics. As a result of the corruption scandal, the PT, formerly the natural occupants of the moral high ground, were utterly discredited. Lula himself was not directly implicated in the corruption but many of the PT's core electorate believe he squandered an important opportunity to change the country's direction.

Of course, as it turned out, Lula defied his opponents and critics by winning a comfortable reelection. However, while Lula went on to become one of Brazil's most popular presidents, the PT never fully recovered. In the context of this widespread political disorientation, one can't help thinking of Junior and his belief in the "Shiva effect": transformation through destruction. It's certainly a philosophy that's well suited to the vagaries of Brazilian life.

When discussing the crisis in the federal government, café commentators are often quick to point out that Brazil has been a democracy for only twenty years. This latest disaster, the argument goes, is one of many on a very steep learning curve. Perhaps they're right. Perhaps, in fact, this is the only sane response. Thinking about the referendum, there's not much that gun control would do to reduce the numbers of illegal weapons reaching the thousands of teenage *soldados* in the city's favelas. After all, most drug traffickers buy their guns from crooked cops.

7

Funk

The *baile*

Late one Friday evening we drive to the Complexo do Alemão. As we pull off the *asfalto* into the favela we're confronted by two large girders protruding from two holes dug into the road. JB honks and they're removed. Apparently these are a new security precaution, installed as a result of the police raid that took place the night Bem-Te-Vi was killed (the night the São Paulo banker got a little more favela reality than he'd bargained for). Not even the feared *caveirão*—police armored car—can get past these.

We're here to meet some people and take in the weekly *baile funk*. We're early, and stop off at a local bar. Out front teams of locals have set up stalls stocking drinks and hot food. Gangs of teenage boys and girls walk up and down, giggling, showing off, flirting. A mild-mannered white guy with pale eyes surrounded by heavy rings stops his high-powered motorbike for a chat. He's carrying a passenger holding a packet of cookies and they look like they've just popped out for a snack. It turns out that, following the death of Bem-Te-Vi, the biker is now the most wanted *traficante* in Rio de Janeiro.

By half past one the huge *galpão** where the party is held is almost full and the crashing sounds of *funk* seem to have taken over the world. The walls shake, the concrete under our feet rumbles, and below, on the dance floor, some two thousand dancers gyrate beneath a powerful strobe. The *baile* is just beginning to take off. JB casts his eyes over the dance, sips a Red Bull, and nods his head. At thirty three, his hard-core *funkeiro* days may be long gone but he knows a good tune when he hears one.

The music is catchy, crude, and hypnotic. In some ways it could be taken as Rio's answer to acid house—repetitive and loud, a way of life to those who know, an easy target to those who don't. The beats are easy to dance to and the rhymes are over-the-top and easy to hear. But communication with anyone else at the *baile* is possible only by shouting at point-blank range, and we soon resort to sign language: "You want a drink?" "She's pretty." "Check out the drunkard!"

We're standing in the VIP area that overlooks the *baile*. We're not "very important," but we are with JB. To the right, a group of young girls try out their routines. The overt sexuality of their movements—thighs spread, backsides gyrating—sits oddly beneath their innocent expressions and occasional bursts of girlish laughter.

Frankly, the whole scene resembles something like a giant (and, admittedly, raunchier-than-average) school disco. In fact, were it not for the small groups of what JB disparagingly calls *viciados*—junkies—snorting furtive lines of coke in the corners, it would be an entirely harmless occasion. Apart from the damage done to your ears.

---

* *galpão*: warehouse-style building used for community events

Besides, the *viciados* are the minority and, to judge by their clothes and demeanor, come from the *asfalto*. These are recreational drug users who come to the *baile* to get high and dance their way into the weekend, not so different from millions of other middle-class youth in hundreds of cities the world over. As for the rest? Their thrills are beer, soft drinks, dancing, and hooking up. Entrance to the *baile* is free and most of the crowd are from the favela with little in the way of spare cash.

Perhaps if we could catch more of the lyrics (predominantly dealing with sex and violence) or if there were armed *soldados* hanging around the dance floor (as there are at many such events), the atmosphere wouldn't seem quite so innocent. Certainly, in the past, the *baile* in Alemão has enjoyed a reputation for serious gangsterism. But nowadays things seem to have changed. The weekly dance is officially licensed by the municipal authorities and it's even filmed for satellite TV. According to JB, the *donos* of several favelas watch these broadcasts later in the week from the discomfort of their jail cells in Bangu, Rio's high-security prison.

The DJ

DJ Marlboro is Rio's most famous *funk* DJ and a household name in Brazil. What's more, the growing international appetite for authentic "Carioca funk" has increasingly seen him travel the globe, and he reels off city names with superstar weariness: "Last week I played in Miami on Thursday, Canada on Friday, and New York on Saturday. Sunday, I was in New Jersey; Monday, San Diego; Tuesday, San Francisco. On Wednesday and Thursday I was in Chicago. Recently I've played at parties in Slovenia, Gdansk, and Amsterdam. I've been to London lots of times." He pauses. "Despite this I earn more playing in Brazil than I do abroad. I work in other countries to spread the culture and open up the market for other artists. When I'm outside Brazil I play the same music as I do here—national *funk*. But I often earn just ten percent of what they might pay me in Rio."

Marlboro has been playing this music since the beginning. It's more than fifteen years since *funk* began to take over the radios, sound systems, and parties of all Rio's poorest neighborhoods and there's no one better placed to detail the history of the scene. He explains that the roots of *funk* date back to the late 1970s and early 1980s, to soul parties held in Rio's suburbs. He cites hip-hop pioneer Afrika Bambaata's electronic anthem "Planet Rock" as a musical turning point: "In 1982, 'Planet Rock' came out and all that electronic music sounded really good on the big speaker stacks. At this time everything electronic was known as *funk*, even what was later to be called Miami Bass."

The first experiments at making a local *funk* sound began in 1988, when producers recorded Brazilian lyrics over imported instrumentals. These were often based on the chants that *funkeiros* chorused at the parties. "There was this Sam Cooke song with the line, 'That's the sound of the men, working on the chain ga-ay-ang.' You know it? And we had a Miami Bass version of that track playing and the people would sing, '*Vem para cama meu bem, vem fazer nene*'—'Come to bed my sweet, come and make some ba-ya-bies.' This came from the *funkeiros*. The songs were in English so the *galera* would invent the chorus."

Marlboro continues: "Within two years people were putting out their own records. And then *funk* became more and more rooted in and made by the communities. The children of *pagodeiros* and *forrozeiros** all began to make *funk*. They tapped into a rich Brazilian musical vein that blends folklore, roots, and knowledge. In turn they began to mix this new music with other cultures from outside. Nowadays the mix of influences you find in *funk* is both regional (within Brazil) and international, too—you'll find samples of the latest stuff from Europe, James Brown, and even Kraftwerk. People make *funk* like they build houses in the favela, using whatever material is available. And nowadays music made in Rio has its own distinct identity, despite being a melting pot of all these other ingredients."

This conversation with Marlboro takes place just after he's finished his daily slot at Rio's FM O Dia, one of the city's top commercial stations. His two-hour midafternoon show is testament to the music's newfound popularity. As so often happens with "ghetto music," the middle classes have now embraced the scene and there are even shows on national TV offering instruction in how to "dance *funk*." Marlboro describes *funk* as "democratic," and it's easy to see what he means, as the growth of the scene inevitably blurs boundaries of wealth, status, and geography. He rates *funk* alongside samba in terms of importance: "In its essence *funk* represents employment, citizenship, and the reintegration of marginalized groups. It's a way for people to express what they feel through music. It's the real Musica Popular Brasileira†—MPB—which expresses the day-to-day lives and thoughts of the people. I don't think anything in Brazil today has as much strength or relates as truly to what people think as *funk*."

---

* *pagodeiros*: fans of *pagode*, the informal parties where samba originated; *forrozeiros*: fans of *forró*

† Musica Popular Brasileira (MPB): the term usually refers to Brazilian pop music of the 1970s and 1980s.

Prohibited *funk*

> "Venho aqui para dizer neste exato momento que o proibidão está liberado para cantar, principalmente também a vocês que gostam de uma boa erva, esta liberado a erva . . ."*

> ("I'm here to say that *proibidão* can now be sung legally, and principally for you who like good herb, that herb is now legal . . .")

While Marlboro, as both pioneer and beneficiary of the *funk* explosion, has every reason to be optimistic, there is also an indisputably dark side to the scene that both taps into and feeds the seamier elements of life in Rio (and possibly even offers part of the explanation for *funk*'s growing popularity).

The most obvious manifestation of this dark side is that it's often the drug factions that promote and finance the *baile*. Their motivations are twofold: first, the parties are popular within the communities, thus securing their power base; second, they draw customers for the drug trade into the favela. But there is also a popular sub-genre of the music called *funk proibido* or *proibidão*—prohibited *funk*—that eulogizes the drug factions, violence, and criminality in general.

Prohibited *funk* is, as the name suggests, illegal, and police try to track down and prosecute its producers. It's been around since the late 1990s and its existence almost exactly correlates with the worst of the interfaction rivalry and turf wars. This is no coincidence. JB says, "I think that nowadays the best way

---

* From the introduction to "President Lula legalises herb," a CV *proibidão* track popular in November 2005

to understand what is happening in favelas is to listen to *proibidão*. The rapper will denigrate the police and promote a particular faction. He'll say that his traffickers have the best weapons and that the best drugs are available in his favela. The rappers tell you the rules of the favela: that rape is forbidden, that you can't steal inside the favela or commit robberies nearby. And they'll tell you what happens to X-9s."

JB should know what he's talking about. His involvement with *funk* stretches back as far as Marlboro's, albeit for very different reasons.

In the late 1980s and early 1990s, *baile funk* was particularly notorious for outbreaks of violence between rival gangs. These were no typical brawls, however, but ritualized fights that were carefully orchestrated by the promoters using hired security to separate the different *galeras* into two sides.

JB tells it like this: "If you can imagine, there'd be two thousand people on each side. Right down the middle there'd be a line of security guards; these great big guys carrying rubber truncheons. This way they formed the famous 'corridor' between the two sides. The DJ would put on different tracks to stoke up the atmosphere and, with each track he played, the atmosphere got a little more rowdy. Then fighting would break out, with the guys at the front punching and kicking the hell out of each other. The security guards would let this go ahead but then, at a certain point, they'd hit us with the truncheons to get us to stop. All of the *funkeiros* would obey.

"You need to understand, these parties were the most important thing for me in my adolescence. I lost teeth and clothes. Sometimes I used to leave the parties with no shoes, my T-shirt all ripped, my face bruised. Sometimes I'd faint."

Nowadays *baile funk de briga*—literally, "fighting *funk*

dances," are largely a thing of the past. After the media began to take note, the authorities eventually managed to close down most such *baile*. There's no record of the number of *funkeiros* killed in this coordinated violence, but celebrated journalist Tim Lopes, for one, put the figure at more than fifty.

The sad irony is that, despite the fighting, these dances were one of the few places in the city where kids from different favelas would mix. But back then the difference between the factions was much less accentuated and therefore disputes between groups from different favelas could be set aside for the duration of the party. In 2005, on the other hand, it's unthinkable that youth from a favela dominated by one faction could attend a *baile* in an area controlled by another. This is not just because of what might happen to them on the night, but also because traffickers from their own community are likely to punish any "traitors" attending a rival faction's party.

The days of *baile funk de briga* also pre-dated *proibidão*. JB admits that he now listens to prohibited *funk* but claims he wouldn't recommend it to anyone else: "Each *proibidão* that the youth makes reflects a reality in the favela. But at the same time they encourage you to smoke, sniff drugs, or even become more violent. For the kids nowadays—I'm not talking about the older guys who are already completely lost—for the younger kids, the music makes them identify even more closely with the faction. This is bad, and I'm definitely against *probidão* for that reason. I listen to a lot of it but I'm against it. And I wouldn't recommend it to anyone, especially children."

Marlboro also is no fan of *probidão* but he's still keen to point out that only a hypocrite would suggest that it doesn't reflect the lives of favela youth. He stresses that prohibited *funk* must not be used to criminalize *funkeiros* and the culture in general: "The government, which doesn't want to take responsibility for problems, blames *funk* for everything that goes wrong. If there's a fight on the beach, it's always blamed on the *funkeiro*. But the fighter might also be a Catholic, a Flamengo supporter, or a *macumbeiro*.* The fact is that it's the government's responsibility to provide policing and security so that people can enjoy themselves. But instead they blame *funk*, a musical movement, for what is essentially their failure."

The key, Marlboro claims, is to work with the MCs and producers who make *funk* and encourage them to use the music as a tool of personal and community development, rather than a celebration of crime and cruelty. "If there was an NGO of *funk*," he says, "no one could control it. *Funk* could be the color of the city, the biggest generator of employment. It would achieve much more than the government does with all its endless projects, projects, and more projects. AfroReggae works, and it's something that was born independently. With the mass movement it has behind it, if *funk* got organized, set up an NGO, and took action inside the community, it would be the most powerful NGO in Rio."

The truth is there are already many similarities between Marlboro's daydreaming and AfroReggae's grand project of social and cultural integration. Just as Marlboro talks enthusiastically of the potential example a successful rapper could set, so Junior lights up when talking about a former *traficante* who's joined one of AfroReggae's bands. Both of them understand the power of music and culture as a force for social change and, while AfroReggae doesn't specifically make *funk*, Junior certainly knows its worth.

The AfroReggae band incorporates *funk* into their sound,

---

* *macumbeiro*: someone who practices Afro-Brazilian religion

and their DJ, Magic Júlio, is something of a *funk* junkie. What's more, Marlboro is a regular feature at Connexões Urbanas and the first single to be released from AfroReggae's new album comes with a *funk* mix by none other than Marlboro himself. Perhaps Malboro's vision of an NGO is, in fact, already being fulfilled.

8

Back in Alemão

Tim Lopes

In 1994, at the tail end of the era of the *baile funk de briga*, a Brazilian journalist called Tim Lopes also went to a *baile* in Complexo do Alemão to research one of an award-winning series of reports he was writing for the Rio newspaper, *O Dia*. On February 27, this is what he wrote: "Here, south of the Equator, in the narrow streets of the Complexo do Alemão the *funk* rhythm . . . is linked to pleasure, letting loose and violence. But *funk* is not just music. It is a way of life. . . . The *funkeiros* own the street, the neighborhood, the city, all of it. They are always ready to win any battle, face anything. . . . In the past three years more than 50 young people have died in fights between *funkeiros*, and hundreds have been injured. The *funk* world has room for sticks, stones and firearms, it embraces nomadic tribes that scatter joy and terror. It is a life-and-death ritual."

Eight years later, on June 2, 2002, Lopes visited another *baile* in Alemão, this time as an undercover reporter for TV Globo. It was to be his last assignment.

Carrying a miniature camera, Lopes intended to film inside the party to expose both the sheer volume of drug-taking and reports he'd heard of traffickers coercing young girls into sex. It was actually the fourth time in quick succession he'd been into the favela. On the first two he checked out the neighborhood, on the third he tried to film but the images weren't considered of good enough quality to broadcast. So he returned one more time. Lopes was due to be picked up by his driver at ten p.m. at the edge of the favela. He never showed up.

Nobody knows if Lopes was recognized from one of his earlier missions or, perhaps, from a report he'd made the previous year in Alemão about the prevalence of open street dealing. Either way, he was discovered by the traffickers and was shot in the leg before being bundled into a car and driven from the neighborhood of Vila Cruzeiro to another called Grota where he was "tried" by the faction and hacked to pieces, his body thrown into a ditch known as "the microwave" and incinerated. It was more than a week before police recovered fragments of Lopes's bones and the charred camera. Elias Maluco ("Crazy Elias"), the *dono* of Comando Vermelho in Alemão, was eventually caught and convicted of the murder.

The killing provoked outrage in the city, the country, and internationally, outrage every bit as vociferous as that prompted by, say, the Vigário massacre in 1993. Angry journalists mobilized. Rosental Calmon Alves, for example, Professor and Knight Chair in Journalism at the University of Texas, devised workshops in Rio just a couple of months later titled "Investigative Journalism: Ethics, Techniques, and Danger," and determined that Lopes's legacy should not be lost. One comment Alves made in an interview typifies the response of the time: "Tim was a journalist in the line of duty, so even if the criminals had not explicitly intended to send a message to all journalists in Rio (and I believe this was, in fact, their intent), they *were* [our emphasis] sending that message. So the attack was not just against one person, but against the press in general, against freedom of the press, which is a basic human right."

Alves undoubtedly has a point. But it's hard not to make comparisons between the rights of the press and the human rights denied every favela resident, like the right to live without fear in a society governed by the rule of law. After all, at least Lopes, though a deservedly respected journalist and, by all accounts, one of the "good guys," certainly knew the risks he was taking and did so by choice.

Whatever you make of this argument, one consequence of his horrific murder is indisputable: If Vigário had once been the Comando Vermelho stronghold, by the time of Lopes's death Alemão already was. If Vigário was once Rio's most notorious favela (courtesy of the massacre), the murder ensured that Alemão now holds this dubious honor. In typical fashion, therefore, AfroReggae sought to expand their work to the complex in the aftermath of the Lopes killing.

AfroReggae's *núcleo*

Drive into Alemão on a bright, sunny morning and the impression you get is not one of exclusion or danger but of a bustling main street alive with business. Wind deeper inside and the road narrows and the shopfronts give way to street football and a first sight of the *soldados*, zipping by on motorbikes, AK-47s strapped across their backs. Deeper still and we come to the *galpão* that housed the *baile*. It's also where AfroReggae is running percussion workshops. The roar of the drums is audible two hundred meters away and, once again, the realization of AfroReggae's oh-so-subtle (and yet not at all) reclamation of space is undeniable.

A curious gaggle clusters around the door, watching— mostly teenage girls holding babies to their hips. The mood is cheerful. JB, ever our guide, takes us to the bar next door for a Coke. Why, then, is the atmosphere so fraught? Perhaps it's because Alemão is geographically set in a basin, its dilapidated shanties rising on all sides around us, offering no escape routes. Or perhaps its because a couple of *traficantes* have taken to idling past, guns bouncing casually against their thighs. Or perhaps it's because JB, as ever our *fiel*,* seems to be sticking a little closer than usual.

AfroReggae actually decided to "invade" Alemão three years earlier, but it took two years of running workshops on the fringes. In the hierarchy of the factions, the *fiel* is a personal security guard and trusted servant of the *gerente geral* of the community (outside the favela) before the organization believed it was the right time to move inside. Unlike a typical faction invasion, AfroReggae has to be a lot more careful. They've only been inside Alemão for a week.

It's JB, as ever, who gives us the lowdown: "Junior came to me with the idea of Connexões Urbanas and I told him there were two communities where we should do it: Morro da Formiga and here in Complexo do Alemão. It was this friendship, this faith in each other, this trust, that started the link. And now we're starting to get the trust of the residents of the whole community, with mothers coming in to ask us questions about what we do. But it's very difficult here because there's nothing but violence and o *tráfico*, so there's an enormous lack of culture.

"We've done a lot of shows in this community in the last few years. Aside from the visits by famous artists like Gilberto Gil, I myself have organized two films to be made here; documentaries about life in the community. So a lot of people here think that everything that happens must be to do with Afro-

---

* *fiel*: faithful

Reggae. Nobody else can come in to do any filming, not after Tim Lopes.

"This is a huge favela, about two hundred thousand residents, bigger even than Rocinha. We have to do something good for these people. We have to play our part.

"There's great exclusion in this community and a very high level of unemployment. Often it's very hard to get a job outside simply because you're perceived as a criminal. But now this community is waking up, showing people it has culture and potential. That is AfroReggae's vision: to show that everyone is equal. Why is AfroReggae known internationally? Because those young men from Vigário were given the chance to show their talents.

"This may be an excluded space but, of course, it sees itself as a community of normal people. It's the people from outside who close themselves off in their little world. How can a young kid in Alemão have an AR-15 rifle while selling cocaine? Who gives that to him? Is there a gun factory here? Is there a cocaine factory here? Of course not.

"Before the arrival of AfroReggae in Vigário, the only thing you'd see about that neighborhood on the news was police brutality, drug trafficking, and negativity. But now? The news you see is all related to cultural projects produced by AfroReggae. It can be the same here. When people think about Alemão at the moment, all they think about is crime. But now? All the people who live here can hear the drums and they know there's something going on and it's good."

The work

We head over to the *galpão* and interrupt the workshop to have a word with Juninho, who is one of the instructors and coordinators of the project. Juninho is from Vigário and he's been in AfroReggae for eight years. Originally a member of one of the subgroups, Makala, he's now a percussionist in the main band. He's twenty-one years old. These workshops are a big deal for the community and a big deal for Juninho, too. It's a lot of responsibility. A stocky character with short dreadlocks and a permanent grin, he is sweating with exertion as he explains AfroReggae's plan.

"The intention is to make another AfroReggae nucleus here in Alemão just like the ones in Lucas and Cantagalo. But it happens very slowly. We've been coming here for two years, but we have only been within the favela for a week. All these kids up on the stage are from here.

"The original idea was a project for thirty students, and one hundred and twenty came to sign up. But eventually some kids decide this isn't for them or whatever and it becomes self-selecting. So this group here are the ones who've shown up to every rehearsal and demonstrated the necessary dedication. Some of them have already begun to go outside this favela to Vigário and Cantagalo for their training.

"The hardest thing for me is teaching students in my same age group. Some don't like to be told what to do by someone their own age. You know how people are in the favela: some like to fool around, some are conceited, some don't like to take orders. I try to say to them: 'I'm from a favela, you're from a favela: We speak the same language.' Because everyone has to understand that we're on the same level. But I must also establish that I am the teacher and they are the students so that we can get things done.

"It helped that I'd been here before for *bailes*, right here in this building, so I already knew people from this community." Juninho gestures toward the stage. "Renato up there? We became friends early on. Eventually, the people who run and coordinate this project will be from Alemão. Renato and Raphael next to him are two of those we have our eyes on as possible leaders. We haven't formed any solid opinions yet, but we think so.

"Junior says AfroReggae is not a franchise and you can't just drop AfroReggae anywhere like McDonald's. We can't just come in and create an illusion and then leave, it has to be a considered and continuous process."

After the rehearsal finishes, we chat to Renato and Raphael. The former is eighteen and a barber, the latter seventeen and still in school. They've both been members of the workshop in Alemão since its inception, although Raphael briefly left to rejoin the traffic. He explains that decision with a shrug. "At one point, our house fell down in bad weather and my family didn't have any way of doing repairs, so I temporarily went back into the traffic in order to make money and help out. I worked as *fiel* for the *gerente*: you know, following him around, storing guns, that kind of thing. It was financial necessity."

Renato chips in: "But we had a word with Raphael and helped him get out again and back in with AfroReggae."

Talking to these two, it's quickly apparent the scale of the challenge AfroReggae faces in this favela; partly because the organization has yet to fully establish a history and reputation in the community and partly because the drug trade is so successful that the *traficantes* earn several times their equivalents in Vigário.

Renato says: "There have been other projects in the favela but they were all directed at kids. There's never been anything like AfroReggae which is actually fun. Of course, the traffic is still very seductive. You see them sitting around the *boca* and they've got all the money and all the girls, so the peer pressure to join them can be very powerful. Like when Raphael rejoined the traffic, the temptation was there for me, too. But it also works the other way round. When AfroReggae came to talk to me, there was pressure on Raphael to come along.

"Sometimes we get criticism from our friends. They'll say, 'What do you want to be doing that for? It's stupid.' But as time goes on and they see what we do, I think we've gained a little respect as well.

"Besides, AfroReggae hasn't just taught us how to play percussion but also how to look at things differently. For example, there's a rival community over the hill, and before we got in with AfroReggae we didn't like them. They never did anything personal against us but we just grew up not liking them and them not liking us. So AfroReggae has opened our minds. We used to be afraid to leave the community, afraid of running into enemies, but not anymore. So now we feel free to go to other favelas and the *asfalto*. AfroReggae has made this happen. It's like a shield."

If the percussion workshops are mostly male, girls are better represented in AfroReggae's Afro-Brazilian dance classes that take place twice each week, and one of their number, Marciana, is currently hanging out and watching the drumming. Marciana is sixteen. When she was ten, her family moved to Rio from Recife in Pernambuco (the northeastern state where President Lula was born—he left there at much the same age as Marciana) so that her father could look for work, and they've been living in the community ever since. She's been training with AfroReggae for two years and talks proudly of the time she performed for Gil in March this year.

We ask her what she'd be doing if she wasn't in AfroReggae. She giggles shyly and murmurs that she'd most likely just be lazing around. What about the boys? This time she answers quick as a flash: "They'd definitely be at the *boca*. All the guys here who have friends in the traffic? Those friends are always trying to persuade them to join."

Marciana explains it like this: "It's different for girls. Guys usually join the traffic at about fifteen, but even much younger boys—seven or eight years old—are already hanging out with the *traficantes*. There *are* women involved, but they're usually girlfriends. A lot of women like to roll with the traffickers because they're rich and they've got all the best stuff. It's a case of the higher rank, the better."

What about you?

"No! I want to stay with AfroReggae and become a dance teacher."

As Marciana wanders back into the *galpão*, JB follows her with his eyes. "The kids here are a little inhibited," he comments. "It's not like Vigário, because here they're not used to outsiders coming into the community to talk to them. Marciana will probably be thinking about that conversation the whole day. It's cool because it all helps to raise her self-esteem."

It's all part of AfroReggae's philosophy: to use every available resource to its fullest to lift the self-worth of its members. So JB escapes *o tráfico* with his life and is now an invaluable resource within the community. So twenty-one-year-old Juninho climbs through AfroReggae's ranks to be entrusted with great responsibility, to which he rises with relish. So Marciana performs for a Brazilian legend and conducts an interview with two sunburned gringos. Maybe she will become a dance teacher.

9

People and Perceptions

In his major work, *O Povo Brasileiro** (*The Brazilian People*), Brazilian anthropologist Darcy Ribeiro describes a country afflicted by three types of conflict: of ethnicity, race, and class. The prime historical example on which he pegs his argument is, once again, Canudos, that Bahian community of freethinkers that was brutally massacred by the Republic's army at the end of the nineteenth century. While Canudos posed no genuine threat to the position of Rio de Janeiro's elite a thousand miles to the south, it did represent an ideological questioning of the merits of the ethnic, racial, and class status quo and, as such, it had to be crushed. This status quo, of course, persists to this day. So, however, does the questioning.

In rural Brazil, it has been taken up by peasant movements like the MST† (landless workers movement) and indigenous tribes like the Guarani and Kaiowá in Mato Grosso do Sul,

---

* Darcy Ribeiro, *O Povo Brasileiro*, São Paulo, Companhia das Letras, 1995

† MST: Movimento dos Trabalhadores Rurais Sem Terra; On December 15, 2005, Federal police evicted hundreds of Guarani and Kaiowá from territory that had been demarcated in their favor by Lula nine months earlier. By upholding an appeal against Lula's demarcation, the Federal Supreme Court ruled in favor of the landowners and against the President.

who must fight tooth and nail for every hectare of land they occupy in the country's interior. In urban Brazil, it has been taken up by the favelas, if not as a coherent "movement," at least in the very fact of their existence. Landless peasants, indigenous peoples, and *favelados* are, in truth, the personification of Ribeiro's conflicts. They are, in the anthropologist's model, the nation's vast population of poor, often described simply as "*clases perigosas*" or "*marginais*"* (literally "dangerous classes" or "marginals").

Luiz Erlanger is the director of marketing at TV Globo, one of the world's largest terrestrial television networks and the primary cultural and political reference for people of all backgrounds across Brazil. He is unsurprisingly erudite, self-confident, and opinionated. He's also extremely generous with his time, pinballing between subjects with verve and wit: We get a condensed history of Brazil, an appraisal of the current political situation, and, of course, the now familiar caveat that it's only twenty years since the end of the military dictatorship.

According to Luiz, many problems in Brazil stem from a self-sustaining political, legal, and bureaucratic dynamic (or rather, perhaps, "undynamic") that restricts change and cripples any hope of progress. For example, thirty-eight parties have politicians elected to a stagnant Congress and no motivation to reform the system that gives them power. For example, in 2004, the UN Special Rapporteur on the independence of judges and lawyers condemned (among other things) the slowness of the Brazilian system, particularly the process of appeals and counterappeals that often seems to grind to a complete halt. For example, small businesses and private individuals operate in a

---

* *marginais* is a word also traditionally used by police to refer to criminals.

regulatory swamp and frequently have to resort to "dishonesty"—
in the form of bribery and so forth—just to make an "honest"
living. For Luiz, it is this all-pervasive acceptance of illegality
that has inevitably created an environment in which crime and
corruption flourish.

"So what does the individual citizen do?" he asks, and then
points in the air. "He goes and lives on the *morro*."

He's talking metaphorically, of course. Or is he? After all,
the favela, though a physical manifestation of the flaws in Brazilian society, can also be, for the individual at least, an illicit
solution.

Next to none of Rio's more than six hundred favelas are
recognized in law and therefore the population of entire urban
areas is defined by the very illegality that, according to Luiz,
holds Brazil back. Indeed, Ribeiro notes that the Instituto
Brasileiro de Geografia e Estatísticas (IBGE)* doesn't even
deign to define favelas; not unless you include favelas in the
extraordinary, pejorative phrase *"aglomerados subnormais"*
("subnormal agglomerations"). The vast majority of the millions of people who make up the *clases perigosas* in favelas and
other poor areas of the city (principally the *periferia*)† are,
therefore, if not actually illegal, then at least in some way beyond the law (by virtue of their residential or work status). And
yet they are also the people who make Rio tick. They work
formally in construction, factories, or on the buses. They work
informally as cleaners and handymen. They work criminally,
selling the pirated goods available on every street corner or, of
course, in *o tráfico*.

---

* IBGE: the national geographical and statistical monitoring body

† *periferia*: literally, "periphery." Suburban areas that, although not designated
favelas, are home to a similar population.

Clases perigosas

So who are these people? One thing you learn about favelas the
more time you spend in them is that no two communities are
the same. Each has its own identity and therefore, in the words
of JB, "its own energy." The character of each favela is rooted
in its racial makeup, social history, and physical location. While
the older favelas that climb the hills of the Zona Sul were often
founded by former slaves, newer communities such as the
sprawling Complexo da Maré (built on reclaimed marshland)
are mostly populated by *nordestino* immigrants. While many
of the zigzagging stairs and alleyways of Cantagalo in the city
center can be reached only on foot, the streets of Vigário Geral
in the suburbs are flat and laid out on a coherent grid, mostly
accessible by car.

The favela population is, for the most part, mixed race. But
what does that mean? Racial definitions are always, of course,
primarily cultural (as opposed to physiological) and, unlike the
historical American white/non-white duality, in Brazil they are
as subtle and complex as all else.

Jailson de Souza, director of the Observatório das Favelas,
a cultural NGO and think-tank based in Maré, explains that the
word *negro* (black) can mean both *preto* (dark black, traditionally a word implying a negative judgment) as well as *mestiço*
(mixed race). He explains that, over the years, interrelations
between black and *nordestino* have created a population that is
primarily mixed race. Nonetheless each favela retains its own
racial peculiarites according to its particular social history.

Jailson makes an interesting point: that class and race divisions operating in the *asfalto* also apply within the favela. "Interracial marriage is more common in favelas but even here
there is racism. In Nova Holanda (in Maré), if you go to the
poorest part of the favela eighty percent of the population is

preto. This is symptomatic of a prevalent racism that operates in Rio. It's harder for *pretos* to get jobs. There's still a racist stereotype that stigmatizes black Cariocas as lazy, while *nordestinos* are supposed to be hard-working."

American writer Marshall Eakin* makes reference to a "well-known" Brazilian saying that goes like this: "We don't have a racial problem here, because blacks here know their place." Like most such sayings, it exists because it contains an element of truth.

Where segregated America, for example, polarized racial definitions as a means to racial control, colonial Brazil had no such luxury, since interracial relationships were not just rife but necessary to populate and work the vast country. Instead, therefore, the nascent culture created a highly nuanced racial hierarchy, which arguably further disempowered those with darker skin. Where African Americans of all hues were lumped together and therefore, ultimately, able to form a discrete racial identity in opposition to dominant white power, darker-skinned Brazilians were only ever engaged in arguments over the bottom couple of rungs of a tall racial ladder.

Indeed, only recently has there been any development of a coherent black identity, and this has largely come about through exposure to other black artistic cultures: African, Caribbean, and African American most of all. Rio hip-hop artist MV Bill, for example, co-founded a black political party, Partido Popular Poder para a Maioria.† Listen to him speak and his language recalls the American civil rights movement, albeit as reworked by African American rappers. Junior's take on the formation of

---

* Marshall Eakin, *Brazil: The Once and Future Country*, London, Macmillan, 1997

† Partido Popular Poder para a Maioria: popular party for power to the majority

AfroReggae is similarly cosmopolitan. He says: "Initially I wasn't really in love with reggae per se but its lyrics and political purpose. It's worth taking note that I was *alienado** at the time. All I wanted to do was throw parties and chase women; so reggae actually helped me in my search for spirituality and purpose. For instance, there was a song saying that Egypt was black. We didn't know that. We thought Egyptians were white because that's what we'd seen on TV. That's why we started dealing with the themes and subject matter of black people in *AfroReggae Noticias*: Malcolm X, Muhammad Ali, great African kings."

It is at least in part due to Junior's "reggae education," therefore, that AfroReggae now specifically sets out to promote black culture and fortify black self-esteem.

Despite economic interdependence and past cordiality, relations between favela and *asfalto* have never been worse. Luiz from Globo blames this on the upsurge of violence related to drug trafficking and the factions' growing power. Jailson from the Observatório, on the other hand, takes a slightly longer view, blaming the Rio state government's wholly unsuccessful war on drugs and lack of social investment for exacerbating the class divide. "I'm forty-five years old," he remarks, warming to his theme, "and I can't recall a more catastrophic experience of a state government than this one. We've had a succession of bad governments, but this is really the worst—because it governs on the basis of a sensationalist populism that is completely ineffective. What's more, its discourse is deeply authoritarian and, as a result of this war on drugs, its public security policy is based on increasingly indiscriminate repression of the poorest communities in the city."

---

* *alienado*: literally "alienated," but also used by Brazilians to mean "politically apathetic"

Local politics

The political field is complicated by the fact that there are three levels of government that exercise power in Rio: the federal government, the state government (to which Jailson referred), and the municipal authority, headed by Rio's mayor, Cesar Maia. Many failures to resolve Rio's historic problems can be traced to disagreements between these three powers and, in 2005, relations showed no sign of improving. In fact, it is reasonable (if depressing) to suggest that the fighting between the strata of government resembles the wars between the three drug factions—it's all about territory, be it physical or political.*

Luiz from Globo tells us a joke that went around the city in the past few months. There was recently an outbreak of dengue fever. When callers phoned a hotline to ask for an insect-spraying vehicle to be sent out, the voice on the other end would ask, "Sir, is that a federal, state, or municipal mosquito?"

When asked to elaborate on the state government's anti-drugs policy, Jailson is lucid. "It's simply a war against the poor based on the argument that drugs must be prevented from reaching users. And what's happened? More drugs are reaching more users all the time; violence, criminality, and insecurity have all increased; and the number of killings of poor adolescents has risen. There is a huge level of police, judicial, and political corruption which has resulted in the state's loss of sovereignty in large areas of the city. This war on drugs has only led to *desgraça* (tragedy)."

In 2005, it's the feared *caveirão*—police armored car—that

---

* The politics of Rio can often seem as nepotistic as they are convoluted. In 2005, the state governor, Rosinha Garotinho, was married to former governor Anthony Garotinho. For the first two years of his wife's term, Anthony served as public security secretary, the position with overall responsibility for policing the state, including the city. Anthony planned to run for president in 2006.

is perhaps the most vivid incarnation of the policy of invasion and repression in favelas. The use of the *caveirão*—by most standards a war machine, of which there are some twelve operating in the city—has already resulted in civilian fatalities.* Jailson sees it like this: "The *caveirão* comes in just to show that the state *can* [our emphasis] if it wants. And it does so as if it were an invading army, shooting in all directions. Anyone could be hit, and then it leaves again. There's no long-term strategy for removal or elimination of the opposing force. It comes in, provokes the *traficantes*, and goes away again. And if the civil population is injured or killed in the process, they're just seen as casualties of war."

Jailson goes on to explain how use of the *caveirão* has created something of an arms race. Young traffickers, enraged by its deployment, are reported to be seeking more powerful weaponry—mortars, flame-throwers, and the like—in an attempt to fight back.

The historic and ongoing failure of the authorities to look for solutions and invest in the long-term social development of favelas continues to worsen the crisis. Even the most basic question of favelas' legal status remains unresolved and calls for favelas—especially, of course, those in Zona Sul—to be knocked down are growing. In 2005, Rio's Public Prosecutor's office presented a petition calling for the removal of fourteen communities, mainly located next to middle-class neighborhoods.

In the meantime, the steady supply of guns and drugs coming into the favelas from outside ensures that the traffickers retain control of the communities. In this way, the technical illegality of the favela is complemented by the actual and continuous

---

* Just one example: in July 2005, Carlos Henrique Ribeiro da Silva was shot dead from a *caveirão* in Vila do João (a favela in Complexo da Maré). He was eleven years old.

criminality of the factions. As long as the traffickers have a stranglehold over these areas, the vicious cycle of violence and repression will only continue and, most likely, get worse.

The consequences

Estimates report that less than 1 percent of favela populations are actively involved in *o tráfico*. Nonetheless, the traffickers' presence is used to justify the criminalization of whole communities. And thus the fear-fueled, media-hyped, historically rooted, phony and yet all-too-real war against the *clases perigosas* continues.

One day we ask Junior whether it might be possible to visit Morro da Providência, Rio's oldest favela, founded by the Canudos veterans. "I don't think that's a good idea," he replies with a shake of the head. Why not? "*Está em guerra*—It's at war." With whom? Junior shrugs: "*Sei lá*—I dunno. The police, I think."

The situation is, bluntly, disastrous. Some organizations— the Observatório, CUFA,* and, of course, AfroReggae—have recognized the valuable role cultural expression can play in promoting social integration, changing the image of favelas and lifting the spirits of their residents. But the state authorities still appear to have other priorities. Jailson gives a pertinent example: "Here in Maré, where there are 132,000 residents, the mayor's office invested 325,000 Reais for us to construct a circus tent and create a cultural space. In Barra da Tijuca in the Zona Sul, where 160,000 people live, they spent 150 million Reais on a 'City of Music.' If this 'City of Music' had been built on this side of town, near Maré, it would not only have pro-

---

* CUFA: Central Unica das Favelas, a hip-hop–based NGO set up by MV Bill

vided employment, but also a place where people from the
Zona Sul could come to mix with people from the *periferia*.
What a wasted opportunity!"

On one of our visits to Vigário Geral, we get into the Afro-
Reggae staff van and there are two teenagers sitting in the back.
Their names are Emir and Marcelo and they're middle-class
kids from the neighborhood to which Jailson referred. Marcelo
watched the film *Favela Rising*, a documentary about AfroReggae seen principally through the experience of Anderson. He'd
never been to a favela before, but wrote Anderson an e-mail
saying how much he liked the movie. Anderson, in turn, invited
him to Vigário for the day. A small gesture maybe, but that day
in Vigário will probably change these middle-class teenagers'
view of Rio for good. While the state authorities appear not to
care about social integration, for Anderson and AfroReggae it's
a key priority.

Toward the end of our conversation with Luiz, we ask him
what he thinks of Junior. His reply is enlightening. "*Finge que
obedece mais manda*"—He pretends to obey but he gives the
orders. We all crack up laughing. Clearly we've all been at
the wrong end of Junior's pointing finger at some time or another. "No, seriously," Luiz continues, "he won't like me saying
this, but Junior does the work of a politician. He has a cause
that he believes in, a job to be done, and he does his best to do
it. That's what I believe a real politician should do."

The Factions

"These days there's not the money there used to be in drugs. The cocaine is *uma porcaria**—of the worst quality. The guys in charge of favelas now are addicts and there are kids getting hooked at ten years old. The only thing they understand is the *boca.* They have no church, no school, and no family so the only institution they belong to is the faction. Drug trafficking in Rio isn't organized crime, the factions are more like football clubs—a mad passion for those involved. All around the world, people fight and kill each other over football, don't they? It's like that."

—*Inspector Marina Maggessi,*
head of the Rio civil police drugs squad

Peace, justice, liberty?†

When JB says he feels unsafe on the *asfalto*, his fear is founded in uncertainty. He thinks that anything could happen at any time for any reason, or even no reason at all. In the favela, on the other hand, there is a set of rules understood

---

* *uma porcaria*: rubbish

† *"Paz, justiça, liberdade"* is a slogan used by the Primeiro Comando do Capital (PCC), a prison-based criminal faction from São Paulo.

by everyone. And these rules come from whichever drug faction commands that particular community.

Three drug factions control Rio's favelas in 2005: the Comando Vermelho (CV), the Terceiro Comando (TC—also called Terceiro Comando Puro), and Amigos dos Amigos (ADA). They share an aim (profit through the drug trade) and have broadly comparable structures at a grassroots level, but they also have different business approaches, superstructures, and guiding philosophies.

While the history and modus operandi of the Comando Vermelho are well documented, there is little available information that illuminates the main distinctions between the CV and the other factions. Using our conversations with ex-traffickers, police, and various experts, therefore, we will briefly try to explain some of these differences. But there is always one caveat: What happens in each favela ultimately depends on how its particular *dono* chooses to run his operation.

In the past, the ADA and the TC have formed manageable working relationships and even alliances. Perhaps this is not surprising. First, they share some practical and ideological attitudes. Second, put simply, each to the other is not the CV. The CV is Rio's largest faction and traditionally its most bellicose.

Whereas the ADA tend to be pragmatists who try to maintain a cordial "working relationship" with the police, the CV undoubtedly regards the police as the enemy, and favelas under CV control are likely to be characterized by shootouts with the cops. As for the TC? They seem to be defined primarily by, if anything, their hatred for the CV.

What most sets the CV apart from the other two factions, however, is its top-to-bottom militaristic hierarchy. The higher ranks of the CV (above the level of any one favela) can give orders that apply right down to individual *soldados* working on the ground. The CV therefore has a clear chain of command, as well as a code of conduct applicable to all members, enshrined in a "statute" agreed upon at an extraordinary meeting of the faction leadership in 2003. By comparison, the TC and the ADA operate more like a cooperative of franchises who look to each other when necessary for support. Favelas controlled by the ADA, for example, share certain ideals and practices but agree not to meddle in each other's internal affairs.

In Rio, the profits from drug sales have been falling for some time. A crackdown on the use of clandestine airstrips has raised the price of interstate transport and thus seen the costs of raw product escalate dramatically. At the same time, corrupt police are charging ever more for protection and, according to JB, in some favelas the factions have been reduced to selling drugs with the sole aim of paying them off. One symptom of this drop in profits is that the factions now appear to be clinging to control of certain areas of the city for reasons of history, prestige, and territory alone. Another is that some former traffickers are turning to kidnaps and bank robberies to earn a living. In the topsy-turvy world of Rio crime, therefore, it is arguable that a lucrative drug trade might make for a safer city, at least in the *asfalto*.

We are told that the decline of *o tráfico* has hit the CV hardest of all. This can at least partly be explained by its confrontational philosophy. Its tactic of always taking on the police and its reputation for extreme violence scare potential buyers away from the *bocas*. Inspector Maggessi puts it like this: "Profit is inversely proportional to violence. The *usuários** won't go

---

* *usuários*: users

where there is violence. So at the CV *bocas*, where you find the craziest kids who are now taking crack, sales are down."*

É nós†

The Comando Vermelho is the oldest and most famous of the three factions. It's said to have originated in the late 1970s when well-educated, middle-class political opponents of the military regime (who had taken part in bank robberies to finance their activities) were held in prison alongside common criminals. In response to the harsh environment, these dissidents banded together with professional kidnappers and bank robbers and taught them a thing or two about solidarity. The result was the foundation of the CV, a criminal organization that initially established codes of behavior designed to protect and control the prison population. As it came to dominate prison life, however, so the CV began to coordinate activities outside: crime money was pooled to support the families of inmates and finance jail breaks.

At the same time (the early 1980s), there was a boom in the domestic cocaine trade and members of the CV were quick to spot the potential for big profits. Several major crimes were committed to finance a calculated step into the drugs business. Small *bocas* were set up in the favelas with loans of drugs and arms, and a network of alliances began to be established. By the mid 1980s, the first generation of armed *soldados* was patrolling Rio's favelas.‡

---

* Crack used to be forbidden by the CV and the other factions. Its emergence in 2005 in Rio's favelas is probably the result of two factors: an attempt to boost falling profits and an alliance between the CV and the PCC. São Paulo is the traditional capital of crack use in Brazil.

† *É nós*: literally "it's us," a CV saying

‡ Source: Luke Dowdney, *Children of the Drug Trade*. Rio de Janeiro: 7 Letras, 2003.

Compared to the chronicled history of the CV, the roots of the Terceiro Comando are altogether more mysterious. It seems it was founded in the late 1980s to challenge the territorial domination of its enemy. The third faction, the ADA, was created in 1996 by a group of breakaway CV members. This moment came about after the murder of Orlando Jogador, CV *dono* of the Complexo do Alemão, by a TC *traficante* called Uê. At the time the two men were the most powerful traffickers in the city and, although they disputed several areas, had declared a truce. This was respected until Uê tricked Jogador into attending a meeting where he was gunned down with a dozen of his *gerentes* and *soldados*. CV *donos* in prison, the story goes, were divided as to what action they should take, and those against executing Uê (who argued that he was within his rights to kill Jogador, who had previously shot and paralyzed his brother) split from the CV and set up Amigos dos Amigos.

The unseen faction?

Luiz Erlanger: "A real investigation would find out who really finances the drug trade, and we know that it's not people from the *morro*, it's people from the *asfalto*."

Hélio Luz, who was in charge of Rio's civil police in the late 1990s, famously said that if people really wanted to fight the drug trade in the city, *usuários* should "stop sniffing in Ipanema"*; he pointed out that he'd never seen armed cops storm the beachfront condominiums to tackle middle-class consumption and dealing.

In Rio, the drug trade run by the factions from the favelas can certainly be a relatively well-paid business and there are

---

* *Para de cheirar em Ipanema*: stop sniffing [coke] in Ipanema. Hélio Luz speaking in the documentary *News from a Private War*.

morros in Zona Sul that run lucrative operations. But there are also numerous communities where turnover is minimal—in Vigário Geral, for instance, 100 grams is regarded as a big sale—and the simple fact is that the trade in most favelas is of small quantities aimed at a local, internal market of recreational users. In terms of the overall volume of drugs passing through the city, therefore, the favela trade is strictly small-time.

So where's the really big money? Who's behind the transfer of drugs in and out of Rio, across Brazil, and for that matter, in and out of the country? A member of the CV is claimed to have made contact in the past with the FARC in Colombia but, even if true, this appears to have been an isolated case.* Is there perhaps an invisible fourth faction involved in national and international trafficking? The stories behind two seizures in particular might answer this question.

In mid-September 2005, federal police intercepted 1.6 tons of cocaine, packed inside frozen meat destined for Portugal. This discovery, one of the largest ever seizures of cocaine in Rio, led to the arrest of several members of *carioca* society in Ipanema and nearby Barra.†

At the time of the arrests, the popular national current affairs magazine *IstoÉ* published an interview with a supergrass who had already testified before two national congressional enquiries into interstate drugs and arms trafficking.‡ From his cell in a police station, Salvio Barbosa Vilar explained how criminals

---

* In 2001, Fernandinho Beira Mar was arrested in Colombia where he was allegedly building contacts with the *Fuerzas Armadas Revolucionarias de Colombia* (FARC), Colombia's largest guerrilla army.

† Along with the drugs, two million Reais were also seized. The money, stored in the federal police headquarters in Rio, was stolen within days. Fifty-eight police were suspended as a result.

‡ "Garganta profunda," *IstoÉ*, September 28, 2005.

used cold-storage food trucks (belonging to well-known national companies) to transport drugs to the cities, then how profits were laundered through high-class restaurants. According to Salvio, who claims he used to drive such shipments, "It's the elite who sustain trafficking. And not just through restaurants. There are other things that are going to come up: supermarkets, motels, and hotels. They've only touched the tip of the iceberg . . . the *quadrilha** is supported by federal deputies, state deputies, judges, and various police commanders and chiefs. Without such support, no *quadrilha* works."

A few months later, at the beginning of December 2005, 500 kilos of cocaine were apprehended in the interior of Pará, an Amazonian state. Who was arrested and subsequently confessed to organizing the shipment? A former mayoral candidate from a municipality in neighboring Tocantins with close links to the PSDB† (former president Cardoso's party) and the Tocantins state government. Though his arrest was hardly covered inside Brazil, it was reported by Reuters and picked up in the international news media. The PSDB moved quickly to expel him.

What do these two examples show us about who is *really* behind the drug trade? Once more, it's probably the strenuously honest Marina Maggessi who summarizes the situation best: "Organized crime has no pact with the factions. It's the upper classes who send cocaine abroad, and what goes on in the favelas has nothing to do with it. There appears to be a huge struggle against narco-traffic going on in Rio but it's really a lie, a great hypocrisy."

---

* *quadrilha*: gang
† PSDB: Partido da Social Democracia Brasileira

Vive e deixe viver*

It's the graffiti that tells you where you are. The uniform, skinny capital letters, designed to stand out from the ubiquitous scrawl of Rio's taggers, seem so similar that, whether they read CV, ADA, or TC, they look like they might have been written by the same childish hand.[†] The letters have one purpose: to let people know who's in charge of a particular neighborhood.

We head to Vila Vintém on the outskirts of the city. This favela is home to Mocidade, one of Rio's most celebrated samba schools, and it's under ADA control. But it looks nothing like Vigário Geral or Complexo do Alemão; in fact, it hardly looks like a favela at all. Nearly all of the houses are painted, the streets are clean and covered in concrete, and there is an air of calm that contrasts with the frenetic energy of other communities we've visited. There are no guns on display, for a start.

We meet with a former ADA *traficante* called Abacate. Now twenty-eight, he was involved for more than a decade and rose to the position of *gerente*. What changed the course of his life? An Urban Connections show where he encountered Junior: by now it's a familiar story.

"When I was a *gerente* I was kidnapped and had to pay the cops numerous times. It got to the point where I didn't want that life anymore. I was too well known to the police. In fact, everyone knew who I was and there was no way I could enjoy myself. I had lots of money but couldn't go anywhere; my movement was restricted to this community. I wanted to learn and expand my knowledge of the world—I love reading and

---

* *Vive e deixe viver*: literally, "live and let live"—an ADA saying

† The letters can be embellished: The CV acronym is often accompanied by the initials RL, in deference to a founding member of the organization, Rogério Lengruber. The ADA acronym is sometimes painted next to a trident, a nod to Macumba, the Afro-Brazilian religion.

finding out about things, particularly religion and politics. Just when I was thinking of getting out I came across AfroReggae and knew that it was what I wanted for myself. I looked at Junior and decided that I was going to follow his path."

Abacate gives us a quick tour of Vila Vintém and his own perspective on the differences between the factions. "There are probably some seventy thousand people living here and maybe zero point five percent of them work in *o tráfico*. All the same, this community has been under the ADA for nearly ten years. *Vive e deixe viver*—live and let live, as we like to say here.

"There are numerous favelas that belong to the ADA, but there's no rigid hierarchy like the CV. The way that it operates in the ADA is that each person is responsible for keeping his own house in order. The guy from here is not interested in what's going on in another favela from a business point of view; they're just friends. If there's a favor that needs doing, then they'll try to help out.

"But in the CV? Today there is one group in charge and that group decides what happens in every community. The TC and ADA don't operate that way. They are divided into separate cells that can each have their own way of thinking that's respected by the others. In the CV it's different. One group makes rules which all the others have to follow. These rules were created precisely because they were scared of losing territorial control and so that certain individuals could maintain power. Their ideology is false. The *cúpula* of the CV is the bourgeoisie of narco-traffic—they're the upper classes and the guys working for them are just plebes obeying orders. For example, you don't have to ask to leave the ADA as long as you don't owe anything. But in the CV there is an internal bureaucracy and usually people who ask to leave are killed."

Of course, Abacate's view of the CV has to be taken in the

context of his past involvement with the ADA, just as JB's opinions reflect his history in the CV. What again becomes clear when talking to both men is the extent to which the two factions have molded their outlooks on life. One can't help noticing subtle ways in which their former membership of a faction influences their behavior: just as Abacate regularly slips into using the word "we" when talking about the ADA, so JB always seems to be wearing a red T-shirt—*vermelho* is very much his favorite color. Inspector Marina's football analogy is entirely apposite. For those involved, faction membership goes way beyond mere crime: it is about the security, values, and self-worth found in group identity.

Peace, happiness, and a bit of knowledge

One of the great successes of AfroReggae is that it bridges the ideological and physical divides that separate factions. In its success and the recognition it has gained, AfroReggae has created a neutral group to which people from all sides of the tracks can belong. Nothing demonstrates this more clearly than the Urban Connections concerts. Not only do Urban Connections draw former key players such as JB and Abacate away from crime and into the AfroReggae family, they also, albeit temporarily, create a neutral cultural space that whole communities can enjoy.

Abacate continues: "AfroReggae's work started with a very simple idea, to help get young people out of *o tráfico*. Then it became this atomic bomb which exploded so that in Rio now all the different communities accept AfroReggae, regardless of faction. Today AfroReggae is perhaps the only cultural organization that can work in any community, be it ADA, CV, or TC. AfroReggae can go into these areas *de cabeça erguida*—its head held high. And it can leave with its head still held high because, the majority of times, it goes out applauded by the *moradores* who, for that moment, are able to forget factions, fights, and wars. They just remember that one group came to bring peace, happiness, and a bit of knowledge."

Guerra

"I never really liked *guerra* [war]. I've been in lots of
shoot-outs with Lucas, because that's what you do. If they
shot at us, I'd return fire until they stopped. There wasn't
as much fighting then as there is nowadays. If you think
about it, it's funny—we call them *alemão* [German] and
they call us *alemão*, too. Germany's got nothing to do
with it."

—*Adriano, ex drug-trafficker from Vigário Geral*

Inspector Marina Maggessi described the factions as "like
football clubs." It's a memorable comparison and one that
gains relevance when you examine the longest-running territorial dispute in the history of Rio's drug conflicts. It was a game
of football that's said to have sparked the twenty-two-year-old
"war" between Vigário and Parada de Lucas.

While the exact details of this game are, unsurprisingly, disputed, the story bears retelling, partly because the "war" is
central to AfroReggae's history and role as conflict mediators,
partly because it highlights the different *modus operandi* of
different factions, and partly because it is a prime illustration
of the chaotic world in which AfroReggae works—a world that
is ever lurching between tragedy and near farce. Mostly, however, what follows provides a response to a question that gets

asked time and again: How is AfroReggae able to operate on all sides of the conflict at once? The simple answer is, by being very careful indeed and at enormous personal risk.

We have heard various versions of what happened from all sorts of people, but here we'll stick with Junior's, since he's the master storyteller. One afternoon in his flat (situated, fittingly, in the same building as the Swiss Consulate), he tells us about the football match and its repercussions. You couldn't, as the saying goes, make it up. . . .

"The residents of Lucas feel hatred for the residents of Vigário and vice versa. Why? The war began in 1983 during a favela football tournament. Vigário and Lucas faced each other in a tense final. It ended in a draw, so there was extra time and then a penalty shoot-out. It came down to the last kick and the Vigário goalkeeper, a guy called Geléia, saved it. There was a pop and he grabbed the ball. All the victorious fans were cheering Geléia, but he didn't get up—he was shot and killed as he dived to save."

Most residents agree it was this incident that began the warring between the two communities that continued unabated for the next decade (and this was before Lucas was controlled by the Terceiro Comando and Vigário became the Comando Vermelho's headquarters). Junior, however, moves on from this unlikely beginning to describe how very different cultures arose in the rival favelas.

Of water parks and torture houses

Junior: "Over the years, Lucas developed more than Vigário through drug sales. In Lucas it was normal to see long queues of buyers and you'd only see a few guns. At the *boca* there were three big bags full of stuff—money, marijuana, and cocaine—and a long queue. I'm talking about the late 1980s and early 1990s.

"At this time, almost the entire leadership of the Comando Vermelho was based in Vigário. The city's most wanted kidnappers passed through and the future *donos* from other favelas were trained and schooled by *traficantes* from Vigário.

"In Lucas, there was lots of money and the *dono* was a great benefactor of the community. His name was Robertinho de Lucas.

"One of the first things he did was paint the whole favela green. Why? Because if the police received information that someone was hiding in such and such a house, it could only ever be 'the green house.'

"If you wanted to set up a business and you had a good proposal and proven experience, Robertinho would become your partner and invest in it. He wouldn't ask for interest and when the loan was repaid he'd leave the partnership. He sponsored local development and people began to make money.

"It was Robertinho who set up a samba school and the first professional football team ever to come from a favela. He even built a water park there at a time when there wasn't such a thing anywhere else in the city.* Thanks to Robertinho, Lucas developed at a terrific rate.

"Unlike other traffickers, Robertinho didn't want war. Traditionally the fighting came from Vigário. Imagine an archipelago of islands: Lucas was one island, circled by a whole archipelago that belonged to the CV. However, over time, Lucas managed to become the strongest of all these islands. It didn't attack other islands, it just defended itself. The favela was developed through drug profits and lots of investment. This is how it happened in the past. These days, after the death of Robertinho, Lucas is an aggressor.

---

* This "water park" still exists. It boasts Olympic-size and learner pools, as well as a water slide.

"Vigário, on the other hand, didn't develop economically, only criminally. Four- or five-year-old kids were growing up with traffickers as idols. There were numerous torture houses where you'd find severed limbs or even the heads of victims hung up as warnings to others. Here's just one example: A *traficante* there dreamed that his girlfriend betrayed him. He quartered her and left each piece on a different corner of the street—just because of a dream. By contrast in Lucas, Robertinho's girl actually did cheat on him and all he did was expel her from the favela. So while Lucas experienced one sort of development, Vigário experienced another, based on terror.

"Then a great icon of *o tráfico* named Flávio Negão arrived on the scene in Vigário. The legend surrounding him says that he was a very religious person, a Jehovah's Witness. Before long he became number one in the favela and attacked several other communities. I remember he was designated public enemy number one by the Rio state government in 1993. It was the first time in my life I'd heard this term. I knew him but we never became friends. You'd hear crazy stories about him at the *boca* reading a Bible, praying, and wearing a T-shirt saying JESUS SAVES. He had a stable in the favela where he kept thoroughbred horses.

"Nineteen ninety-three was the police massacre in Vigário. Robertinho de Lucas was so affected by it that he proposed a peace deal that lasted seven years. There was also an excellent operation carried out by the police in 1996. Without firing a shot, they managed to stifle trafficking in both communities and even managed to win the trust of the *moradores*. But then, in 2000, Cuco attacked Lucas and the war began again more ferociously than ever. Robertinho de Lucas was killed a few years ago by one of his own men.

"More and more people grew to hate the other side. Children

as young as five or six see members of the other community as enemies. Hate starts very early."

Eighteen days of peace

"AfroReggae mediates between Vigário and Lucas and we've succeeded in achieving a ceasefire, something that had never been done before. One afternoon in August 2004, when we were trying to negotiate this, I was in Lucas speaking to its current *dono* [after the death of Robertinho] near the frontier between the two communities. All of a sudden my phone rang. It was Vitor,* asking where I was. When I told him I was in Lucas, he said he'd phoned to tell me that the *traficantes* from Vigário were planning to invade. Why? In retaliation for an attack the TC had carried out the week before.

"I was standing next to the *dono* of Lucas. Vitor was standing next to the *gerente geral* of Vigário. He passed him the phone and I asked why they were going to attack right now. He said, 'Shit! Those guys are sons of bitches, cowards. We're going to kill everyone!'

"Of course, the boss from Lucas is standing by my side and can hear everything. So I say to the guy from Vigário, 'Speak to him. He's here now.' And I pass the phone over.

"Their conversation was so polite, they sounded like two orchestra conductors exchanging pleasantries. I even heard the *dono* of Lucas saying to his counterpart in Vigário, 'Man, I respect and admire you.'

"The boss of Lucas then had the unfortunate idea for all of us to go and meet on the front line. The front line is a street— there's a school there (the Brizolão), and a police post (where the cops are completely corrupted)—with Vigário on one side

---

* Vitor is coordinator of the AfroReggae nucleus in Vigário Geral.

and Lucas on the other. I was there with Anderson, JB, the AfroReggae coordinators from Lucas, and some seventy traffickers all armed to the teeth. On the other side there were about seventy traffickers from Vigário, Vitor, and LG.* At this point the police took off, terrified.

"We stood there looking at each other for a while and I decided to cross to the other side. Whenever I mediate in conflict situations I try to keep a song in my mind, usually something from a film. It helps me keep cool and focused. I crossed the frontier and guess what song came into my head? 'Sunday, Bloody Sunday' by U2.

"For some reason the Vigário traffickers didn't recognize who I was and aimed their guns at me. But I had to keep walking and, when I glanced to my right, I saw all the kids in the school crouching down with the teachers. Everything had stopped at this point as this was completely out of the ordinary. Generally, on the front line, someone shoots a couple of rounds and then ducks behind a wall. To have groups of seventy squaring up is not normal.

"The first thing that happened when I got there was that the boss of Vigário gave me a hug. I said to him, 'Listen, we're going to put on a theatre production here. I want peace.' We actually did put on a Shakespeare play there which more than two thousand people came to see.†

"'You want peace?' he asked, and then dropped his gun and walked over with me, putting his life in my hands, something I hadn't asked for.

"So we walked across no man's land to the point that

---

* LG is a singer in the AfroReggae main band.

† This was a performance of *Antony and Cleopatra*, put on in conjunction with TV Globo and People's Palace Projects, a UK-based NGO, as part of a series of events involving members of both communities called "Parada Geral."

divides the two favelas. We went there together and the *dono* from Lucas came to meet us.

"They shook hands and hugged: 'It's sealed—a ceasefire for the AfroReggae theatre piece.' Thus began an eighteen-day truce, even though it was only supposed to last for a few days.

"This is a story that apparently has a happy ending and I'd have liked it to be that way. But don't forget that these communities have been fighting for nearly twenty-five years. Two months later, Lucas invaded Vigário with an army of some two hundred men that included Terceiro Comando *traficantes* from other favelas. Vigário wasn't expecting anything, so there was no attempt to retaliate. What made matters worse was that the invaders were accompanied by a group of residents from Lucas. They had a worse attitude than the *soldados* and began to loot houses and attack innocent *moradores*."

Invasion

"In 2004, when Lucas attacked, the trafficker in charge of the operation was a childhood friend of Anderson. This was the same guy who killed Robertinho de Lucas even though he was from the same faction, the one who'd made the peace deal.

"Why does he have good relations with AfroReggae? When he was a child he used to go hungry and Anderson's mother, who worked in a school in Lucas, set aside food for him to take home. She would never have imagined that this child would become a *dono* in the traffic but now he's crazy for them both. Sometimes, when Anderson went over there, he'd decorate the streets with flags and treat him like royalty. He loves Anderson. He's also the number one in Lucas and has a lot of power.

"When the Terceiro Comando invaded Vigário they paid the police 200,000 Reais not to intervene. Residents fled their houses, which were ransacked. Imagine ransacking the houses of people who have nothing?

"There's a scene that sticks in my mind. Someone who used to work for us had just done his grocery shopping for the month. He'd bought Nike shoes, which he was going to pay off in installments, and a whole bunch of Danoninho yogurts for his kids. He's poor, and whoever ransacked his house broke open the tops of each Danoninho and threw them on the floor. Everything he'd bought had been stolen. He was so full of hate that he couldn't communicate at all. The traffickers came back to his house and started asking him questions but he couldn't speak. They tied him up and took him away. They didn't kill him only because his cousin, Dada, arrived in the nick of time. The traffickers respected AfroReggae and let him go.

"This all began on a Saturday, October 2, and there was only one person who could control this situation: Anderson. He went to Vigário along with Altair and Dada* to start taking on the invaders. There were different rumors every few minutes—that so and so was being tortured, or that they were going to kill someone else. Anderson had to follow up every one to confirm what was happening, because he was the only person who could move around safely.

"On the next day, there were elections all over Brazil. The people in Vigário couldn't vote even though it's obligatory. Anderson began to run out of energy and patience with the head of trafficking in Lucas and asked what he was doing.

"Then, the Vigário mob who'd already left the favela began to spread a rumor saying that Anderson had helped the invaders because he was a friend of their boss. After all, the first

---

* Dada and Altair are percussionists in AfroReggae's main band.

thing the *dono* had done when they invaded was go to Anderson's mother's house and give her a kiss. In doing this, he fucked things up for both Anderson and his mother.

"Until then, I'd been mediating from outside. But the next day Anderson was really fed up so we took him out for a while and I went to Vigário.

"I sat down for separate talks with the two bosses. It was very tiring. The *dono* of Lucas doesn't like me and he's scared of the media AfroReggae can get. I know a lot of traffickers from all the different factions, but him I don't trust. His contact in AfroReggae is Anderson, not me. Then later, while I was trying to calm down the *traficantes* who'd fled Vigário, a veteran CV trafficker came by and said, 'Listen. I'm going into Lucas and I'm going to kill everyone. I don't care, I'm going to kill residents, children, old people, whoever.' It was exhausting. I went home and sent an e-mail to various people, including Damian at Amnesty International in London.

"On Thursday, the boss of Lucas called and said, 'Junior, speak to Anderson! He's giving me problems!' By now, Anderson was arguing with the armed invaders, shouting at them and giving orders. We were upset because they'd scrawled the symbol of their faction over walls we'd painted with graffiti. Writing the name of the faction on AfroReggae murals was a gigantic offense. It was our art and it wasn't right for them to do that. But the *dono* told me: 'If he [Anderson] keeps on going like this, I'll beat him up in front of everyone.'

"I began to get desperate. The police appeared on television saying the situation was under control. This was a lie, as they'd never tried to take on the traffickers from Lucas. But then we got the break that we needed. Damian phoned and said that he was going to write a press release based on the e-mail I'd sent. I asked him to emphasize that the authorities weren't doing anything. On Friday the Amnesty press release hit the front pages and international wires. Finally the BOPE were sent in.

"When they arrived there was an incredible argument between the BOPE and the local military police. The BOPE screamed at them in front of everyone: 'You sons of bitches! You've been paid off, done fuck all, and now we've got to go and risk our lives!'

"The most incredible thing was that this was true. During the previous week, you could have seen corrupt police openly playing cards and drinking with the Terceiro Comando traffickers in Vigário. They were even listening to *funk proibidão*.

"In the end two hundred BOPE came in and killed seven or so traffickers, driving them out of the favela.

"If the gang of residents from Lucas who came in with the traffickers hadn't been so disgraceful—looting and so on—Vigário might still belong to the Terceiro Comando today. But they were worse than the criminals. When the residents of Vigário went back to get their stuff, whatever was left, even then they were prevented from doing so by the residents of Lucas. And the police were too busy chasing the traffickers to do anything about it.

"What I've told you was basically a prelude. Now it gets worse."

Mediators

"During all this confusion between the *moradores*, Anderson, Vitor, Altair, and Dada tried to stop them fighting. But there were fewer residents of Vigário, so the people from Lucas began claiming Anderson was on the Vigário side. One in particular started giving him real grief so Anderson invited him out for a fistfight. This man didn't want that. Instead, he went back to Lucas and spread a lie. He said that Anderson had kidnapped twenty *moradores* from Lucas, that he'd raped a girl, that he was brandishing a gun and threatening people from Lucas. Even though this was ridiculous, people believed it. Then the police kidnapped the *dono* of Lucas (to earn some money), so Anderson had lost his friend and protector.

"By now, early on Friday evening, seven people from Afro-Reggae were stuck in the middle of all this and the BOPE had gone. I set off to try and negotiate with a boss of the Terceiro Comando in another favela and got stuck in a traffic jam. At the same time, a crowd of people from Lucas armed with guns, rocks, and sticks had gathered where Anderson was. He called me and I listened to all the yelling and shouting. I turned back to Vigário, prepared to die with my friends.

"I had two phones with me; on one I was listening to the scene in Vigário and on the other I had a trafficker from Lucas saying that if he saw anyone from AfroReggae with a gun, he'd kill them. This made me both more anxious and more calm because I knew that no one in AfroReggae had guns.

"I kept on listening to what was happening. Anderson, Altair, and the others went on the offensive, arguing with the mob and pointing their fingers in their faces. They got worked up into a kamikaze frame of mind and refused to back down. Even though the people were all armed and, obviously, they were scared, they didn't show any fear. It was all a front as they shouted: 'Get fucked! Fuck you!' The gang in front of them wasn't expecting that, and the crowd calmed down.

"I was nearing Vigário. Up to this point I'd heard everything, but then my phone cut out. When I got there I expected to find dead bodies. Instead, I found my friends celebrating their survival. Despite the chaos around them, they'd managed to mediate and turn the situation around. Some of the traffickers from Lucas had even apologized.

"The favela was like a ghost town. But while we were celebrating, thinking that the story was over, we found out that it wasn't. I was told that people in the CV from Vigário had issued a death sentence on Anderson. So on Friday the Terceiro Comando wanted to kill him, and on Saturday, the Comando Vermelho wanted to. So once more we had to take him out of the favela. Me and JB then went around a whole load of places trying to talk to different people.

"Things became seriously absurd when the real bosses in Bangu prison heard about this latest development. These are the top men in the CV and they pronounced an immediate death sentence on anyone who touched Anderson.

"Sometimes the way they view AfroReggae surprises me. The letters they send me are like fan letters. They say how much they like AfroReggae and that, if they had a chance, they'd like to join to change their lives.

"Finally, when the order from Bangu was put out, Anderson was safe. The whole saga had exhausted us all and I felt it would be the last time we tried to mediate a conflict. What amazes me is that, since then, we've carried on trying to mediate. In fact, I'd even say we're a thousand times more keen now."

12

How It Works

Leida, the maid at our *cobertura* in Copacabana, told us a story about her nephew. He was hanging around outside a bar beneath their house in Rocinha when he was called over by a drug trafficker. Luckily her husband was there and, as he knew the *traficantes*, he was able to keep the boy out of trouble. But what if he hadn't been there? What might have happened?

We've made up the story that follows to illustrate the factions' local structure and the way a young *traficante* can climb the hierarchy. If you've seen the films *Cidade de Deus* (*City of God*) or *Notícias de Uma Guerra Particular* (*News from a Private War*), some of the events will probably seem familiar.* Let's take another kid in another favela. We'll call him Jorge. He's eleven years old. Jorge lives with his mother, Adriana, but he doesn't see much of her because she's holding down two jobs in her struggle to maintain their household. She leaves home every morning at five a.m. to clean offices downtown before heading on to the factory on the other side of the city where she works

---

* *Cidade de Deus*, directed by Fernando Mereilles and Kátia Lund, 2002; *Notícias de Uma Guerra Particular*, directed by Kátia Lund and Joào Moreira Salles, 1999.

on the production line. Jorge is mostly cared for by his grand-mother. She's elderly and has been sick for a while so she can't keep an eye on him as closely as she'd like to.

Jorge goes to primary school in the community. He's a good footballer and, after school, he usually plays with his friends. Mostly they have a kick about in the street outside his house, but sometimes, if the older kids aren't using it, they get to play on the rough-and-ready, five-a-side pitch near the edge of the favela. The faction that runs the drug trade in this favela have a *boca* right next to the pitch. The *traficantes* often have a sound system at the boca that blasts *funk proibidão*. The footballers like it when there's music. It almost feels like there's a crowd watching. They soon know all the words to every track.

One Christmas, the *gerente de boca*,* a sixteen-year-old named Marcelo, pulls up on his motorbike with his girlfriend sitting behind him. He's wearing a gold chain and all the best clothes. He's got a 9mm pistol poking out of the back of his shorts. He gets off the bike, swaggers right into the middle of the football match, and produces a wad of banknotes from his pocket. All the players gather round. Marcelo says, "In the faction we look out for the local kids." And he tosses a bunch of small-denomination bills onto the ground. Jorge and his friends scrabble to grab what they can.

Not long afterward, during another game, Jorge scores a brilliant goal. Marcelo is watching from the *boca* and calls him over. The *gerente* tells him he's the best player and asks if he's trustworthy, too. Jorge says he is, so Marcelo gives him 20 Reais and sends him to a nearby bar to buy food for all the *vapores*†

---

* Each *boca de fumo* has a manager responsible for the sales of marijuana and cocaine.

† *vapor*: one who sells drugs directly at the *boca*

at the *boca*. When he gets back, Marcelo lets him keep the change. Soon it's a regular occurrence for Marcelo to send Jorge on small errands. Sometimes he buys food or drinks, sometimes he takes messages to Marcelo's girlfriend or other *traficantes*. The *gerente* always gives him a little bit of cash and the *vapores* get to know him and start treating him like one of the gang. Jorge has become an *aviãozinho*.

Olheiros*

A few months later, Marcelo summons Jorge as usual but this time he calls over Jorge's best friend, Ignácio, as well. This time, Marcelo is sitting with his direct boss, César, the *gerente de branco*.† He tells them that he needs two new *olheiros* and he wants to know if they're up to it. They both say yes without a moment's doubt.

Their first job is as *fogueteiros*.‡ They're stationed on rooftops in the outskirts of the favela and given fireworks to set off if they see cops or *soldados* from an enemy faction. It's boring work but they're paid 100 Reais a week each. Jorge is already earning as much as his mother. Ignácio starts to smoke a lot of *maconha* to pass the time, but Jorge doesn't like the taste of it.

Jorge now stays out of his house until all hours of the night and it's not long before Adriana figures out what's going on.

---

* *Olheiros*: lookouts stationed at key points throughout the *favela*. They are often equipped with radios, to warn of invasions by the police or other factions.

† The *gerente de branco* is responsible for overall cocaine sales in the community. Also known as the *gerente de cocaína*. An equivalent rank is the *gerente de preto*, responsible for marijuana sales (also known as the *gerente de maconha*).

‡ *fogueteiros*: literally, "fireworks." These *olheiros* are equipped with fireworks to warn of invasions.

She confronts him and demands that he stay away from the *movimento*:* Does he want to be dead or in prison before he's eighteen? Jorge listens sullenly but he doesn't take any notice. He's getting well paid and the *traficantes* are like his brothers now. When he's not in place as a lookout, he spends all his time hanging out at the *boca*. He doesn't play football anymore. That's kids' stuff. He's stopped going to school.

One evening, when Jorge and Ignácio are on duty, there's trouble. Twenty armed *soldados* from an enemy faction are taking up positions on the front line, ready to invade. Ignácio's been smoking all day and he's high but, fortunately, Jorge is alert and sets off his fireworks—*PAP PAP PAP!* He grabs Ignácio by the arm and they clamber across the rooftops of the favela, heads down, looking for cover. In the streets below them they can see the *moradores* scattering for cover, the grilles on shop fronts slamming down, and a dozen *soldados* from their own side rushing toward the front line brandishing AK-47s. Then the shooting starts. The *alemão*† have invaded.

The two boys drop onto a corrugated iron shack and then into the alley below. The gunfire is close by. Ignácio is scared and ducks into the shadows and away. Jorge's scared, too, but he's exhilarated and, in spite of himself, he heads up the alley toward the street where the gun battle is raging. At the corner, the *gerente de soldados*,‡ a nineteen-year-old known as Blanco who's famous for his bravery, is shooting off round after round from his AR-15.

---

* *movimento*: "movement": another word frequently used to refer to *o tráfico*

† *alemão*: literally, "German." The word used by traffickers and members of the community to mean "enemy," typically members of other factions or the communities from which they come.

‡ The *gerente de soldados* is responsible for armed security within the community.

The local *traficantes* are outnumbered and are being pushed back. Blanco hands Jorge a Glock automatic pistol and points him up to a spot on the low roof above them. Jorge is too small to get up there on his own and Blanco has to give him a hand. Jorge realizes he could be hit at any moment but, as soon as he's in place, he feels a little better. He's never fired a gun in anger before, but he's been around long enough to know the drill. He holds himself steady and shoots for the first time.

It's forty-five minutes before the invaders retreat and the *traficantes* celebrate by firing into the air. Two of them have been hit. One is carried to a nearby house to have his leg wound treated, the other is César. When Jorge looks down at the body and the bloody mess where the *gerente de branco*'s left cheek used to be, he doesn't know what he feels. Part of him feels sick, but there's adrenaline still coursing through his veins. Most of him feels nothing at all and it's that nothingness, that emptiness, that disconcerts him. He wonders what he's supposed to feel.

His faction has killed three of the enemy. A fourth is lying flat out in the middle of the street with blood seeping from a stomach wound. The local *traficantes* are gathered around him as the boy, maybe sixteen years old, struggles to stand up, as though, if he managed it, everything would be OK and he'd be able to walk home.

Some of the *soldados* start to mock their dying enemy. One stamps on his hand, another on his crotch. Blanco is standing next to Jorge. He tells him to kill the *alemão*. Jorge shoots him in the head without hesitation. All the boys laugh and cheer. Blanco pats him on the shoulder and tells him he can hold on to the Glock on loan from the faction. Jorge nods. Again, he finds he feels nothing. He's just turned thirteen years old.

Vapores

In the aftermath of the battle, the *gerente geral** of the faction promotes Marcelo to *gerente de branco* to replace César. Marcelo comes to see Jorge and Ignácio. He tells them that they are "*preparado*"† and it's time they took more responsibility. They, in turn, are promoted and become *vapores* at another *boca*. In a good week, they could earn as much as 350 Reais.

The *gerente* of this *boca* is a guy known as Lula on account of his resemblance to the president. Lula is a thickset boy of seventeen who's also new to his position. It's all change in the faction hierarchy.

These days, Jorge is hardly ever at his house, but one day he comes home to find his uncle, who lives on the other side of the favela, standing in the small kitchen with his mother. Clearly she intends a showdown.

Adriana begs him to leave the *movimento*. She tells him that she hasn't worked so hard for so long to see him throw his life away. His grandmother starts to cry. His uncle, who works as an electrician within the favela, tells him that he can take him on as an apprentice and pay him an honest wage of 250 Reais a month. Adriana follows up by telling him that, as much as she loves him, she won't have a *traficante* living in her house. Jorge doesn't need this. He's got problems of his own. He throws his few clothes into a bag. Before he leaves, he pulls 500 Reais out of his pocket and gives it to his mother. He goes to stay in a house with other *traficantes*.

One of Jorge's problems is that he doesn't get along with

---

* *gerente geral*: The general manager of *o tráfico* within the community, reports directly to the *dono*. Also known as *segunda voz* (second voice).

† *preparado*: initiated (literally, "prepared"), used to describe someone ready to take a full part in the faction

Lula. Another is that Ignácio seems to have become Lula's best friend. Jorge thinks that Lula is a show-off. He's always splashing cash around, wears silver studs in his ears and a silver cross at his neck. He's always got a different girl on his arm and he's always last to leave the *baile*. This is all fine but he neglects his duties: he doesn't check the *cargas** from the *endoladores†* and he'd rather talk to all his different women than keep an eye on the *olheiros*. *Vapores* work on commission, and a neglectful *gerente* means fewer sales, so Jorge is earning less cash. He finds himself taking on a lot of Lula's responsibilities to make sure the operation runs smoothly. He considers speaking to Marcelo but doesn't want to be disloyal, and besides, his best friend, Ignácio, is smoking more and more *maconha* and seems to have become Lula's lackey.

It's a quiet midweek afternoon when it all goes wrong. Jorge and Ignácio are at the *boca*. Lula is elsewhere as usual. Ignácio is high as usual. There's no warning from the *olheiros*, and the first they know of the police incursion is when the *soldado* standing next to them is shot dead. The *soldado* instinctively squeezes the trigger of his AK as he falls and two local kids playing football are shot in the ankles and feet.

Ignácio drops his revolver and flees deeper into the favela. Jorge grabs the *cargas* and the cash and follows him. As he runs up one of the community's main streets, Jorge is vaguely aware of the people taking cover around him and of gunfire, of course. Jorge shoots blindly over his shoulder. The BOPE are close.

Jorge sees Ignácio still running as he ducks into the nearest house. Inside, the *moradores* are lying on the floor, their hands over their heads, but Jorge takes no notice of them. He sprints

---

* *cargas*: literally, "cargo"; quantities of drugs wrapped up in small paper parcels

† *endoladores*: those employed by the faction to package the drugs

up the stairs, out of a window and across the rooftops. Behind
him, he hears BOPE gunshots from the house he's just left but
he takes no notice of them and he doesn't think about whom
they might have hit. He has to get away.

He jumps down into a small yard and hides under a tarpau-
lin sheet. It's less than a minute before he hears the police
prowling above his head. Jorge's heartbeat is so loud that he
can't believe the cops don't hear it, but he holds his nerve and
before he knows it, their radios crackle and they're called elsewhere. Still, it's ten minutes before he dares move.

He climbs back onto the nearest roof. The first thing he
sees, in the distance, is Ignácio in handcuffs being led up a hill
at the back of the favela by two policemen. It's a familiar scene:
a crowd of *moradores*, women especially, are following them,
willing witnesses for one of their own community. If the police
get a *traficante* alone, anything could happen.

Behind the two cops holding Ignácio, another pair tries to
persuade the procession to disperse with a mixture of sweet
talk and threats. A teenager Jorge recognizes as one of Ignácio's
girlfriends from the *boca* runs forward and grabs a policeman
by the shirt, begging him to let the boy go. He slaps her to the
ground and, after that, the *moradores* slow and finally halt
before the cops' guns. For a moment or two Jorge can still see
Ignácio. Then he disappears behind a building at the very top
of the favela.

Then the favela is silent and still. Jorge thinks it's like someone's pressed the Pause button. Opposite his position, on the
other side of the street, there is a window box in full bloom.
Jorge can see a hummingbird hovering, apparently motionless,
its beak in one of the flowers. When the two shots ring out
from the top of the favela, the hummingbird is gone. It's back
in position a couple of seconds later.

Jorge can see the BOPE coming down through the favela, carrying Ignácio's body. He hears women screaming and wailing. He fingers the butt of his pistol. Maybe he can shoot a cop another day. Ducking out of sight, he sits down on the roof with the cocaine and the money and waits for the coast to clear.

Eventually Jorge heads down into the street. He runs straight into Blanco, who seems angry: "Where have you been?"

"I was hiding."

"Have you got the stuff?"

"Of course."

"Come with me. Mota wants to see you."

Mota is the *gerente geral* and Blanco leads Jorge up through the favela toward the very place where the cops shot Ignácio. Jorge starts to feel scared because everybody knows that this is where executions happen—for police and *traficantes* alike.

At the spot, Mota is with Marcelo and two *soldados*. One of the *soldados* takes Jorge's gun. Mota is a lean, lanky twenty-three-year-old with narrow eyes, an utterly unreadable expression, and a slow, sleepy voice. Lula is there, too, shifting from foot to foot, looking nervous and edgy.

The point where they're standing overlooks a ravine that drops steeply into some woods and then, below that, to the *asfalto*. Some curious kids have hidden behind a nearby building to watch what happens. Marcelo goes over and tells them to beat it.

Marcelo takes Jorge's bag—the *cargas* and the cash—and peers inside. He whispers something to Mota. The boss nods.

Mota tells Jorge that they have a problem. Ignácio is dead, the *soldado* at the *boca,* too. What's more, two kids were hit in the crossfire at the *boca* and the cops killed one of the *moradores* in the house through which Jorge fled. All of this could

have been avoided, Mota says, if they had been properly organized.

Jorge looks at the ground as he explains there was no warning of the police invasion from the *olheiros*. Mota asks why not.
The young *vapor* shrugs. Mota asks where Lula was while all
this was going on. Again, Jorge shrugs: "I dunno."

Mota says quietly, "It's not good enough."

Jorge looks up to find the *gerente geral* pointing his own
gun, the Glock pistol, right at him. His heart catches in his
chest. He glances at Lula, but Lula won't meet his eye.

What happens next is too quick for Jorge to process. One
of the *soldados* is holding an AK and, without warning, he
slams the butt into Lula's cheek and the *gerente de boca*
crumples to the ground. Where, a moment before, Mota was
pointing Jorge's own gun at him, now he's holding it out and
saying, "Take it." Jorge takes the pistol and finds comfort in
the weight of it in his hand.

Lula is just getting to his knees. Mota gestures at him dis-
missively and says to Jorge, "Kill him." Jorge hesitates. Lula
looks up at him and starts to cry. Then he pukes in the dirt.
Mota says again, "Kill him." And this time Jorge lifts his gun
and shoots the boy in the back of the head. He falls forward
into his own vomit. The two *soldados* drag the corpse to the
edge of the ravine and drop it over.

Landing in some bushes twenty meters below, it disturbs
some nesting birds that take flight until they're level with the
traficantes. Their screeching song sounds like laughter.

"Good," Mota says, to no one in particular. Then, directly
to Jorge: "That's what happens when you don't run business
efficiently: people die. Hold out your hand."

Mota extends a fist to the younger boy who does as he's

told. He feels something hard and cold drop into his palm. It is Lula's silver cross. Jorge is promoted to *gerente de boca*. He's not yet fifteen.

A simple statistic

It is worth reiterating that stories like this unfold in Rio's favelas on a daily basis. This is a war zone. Here is a simple statistic that may illuminate the level of violence: Between 1948 and 1999, an estimated thirteen thousand people were killed in the Israeli–Palestinian conflict. Between 1979 and 2000, more than forty-eight thousand died from firearm-related injuries in the city of Rio.*

---

* Source: Luke Dowdney, *Children of the Drug Trade*. Rio de Janeiro: 7 Letras, 2003.

13

The Police

Cultural invaders

I t's eleven a.m. on a Tuesday and we're sitting in a classroom in Rio's Candido Mendes University with a group of AfroReggae instructors. They have recently returned from Brazil's third largest city, Belo Horizonte, and they're evaluating the series of workshops they ran in street ball (a type of basketball), graffiti, theatre, dance, and percussion. They're young, engaged, and give every impression that they learned a lot from the experience.

The drama instructor describes how difficult it was to get the participants to relax and join in. She found it hard, for example, to persuade them to look one another in the eye. "They didn't seem to have much confidence. One of them actually said, 'Damn! You're going to have to blindfold me because I don't even trust myself.'"

The graffiti instructor, an enthusiastic type with the name Chico tattooed graffiti-style on his arm, says it was the talent of his students that really surprised him. One of them, however, refused to write his initials next to what was possibly the very best piece.

Why these problems? Perhaps the answer lies in the identity of the students. What was so unusual about the participants in these workshops is that they were not former *traficantes*, or even marginalized favela youth, but military police.

Silvia Ramos, of CESeC,* the policing and public policy NGO that devised the project alongside AfroReggae, describes how it worked. "The basic idea was to open up channels of communication between the police and youth from the communities they work in by introducing them both to the instructors and cultural elements of favela life, and to do this without forcing them to compromise their professional identity. At the same time we wanted young people to grasp the similarities between themselves and the police. How could this be achieved? By putting on these training events inside police stations. We call them cultural invasions."

The project was devised in 2002, partly because AfroReggae had endured numerous run-ins with the police and partly because Junior was repeatedly asked why AfroReggae only helps *bandidos*. The initial intention was to make it happen in Rio but, after some discussion, this was rejected by the authorities. Plans were then put on hold until mid-2004, when the security secretariat and military police of Minas Gerais asked AfroReggae to come to Belo Horizonte. It is depressing, if perhaps unsurprising, that none of these instructors thinks it would be possible to bring the training back to Rio right now.

"The police in Minas are different," says Chico. "They have a completely different culture and way of operating. We couldn't work with the Rio police in the same way."

AfroReggae's cultural invasions address an issue all too often overlooked by human-rights organizations, governments, and the general public—that the police themselves, the military

---

* CESeC: Centre for Public Security and Citizenship Studies

police most of all, typically come from some of the poorest sectors of society. The simple fact is that young people often go into the force for exactly the same reasons a teenager might be drawn into trafficking—lack of money, lack of alternatives, and a substandard education. An advertisement for four thousand vacancies in the military police recently drew thirty-seven thousand applicants, despite the fact that Brazil's police are notoriously poorly paid, badly equipped, and undertrained.

There are three principal police forces in Brazil. Uniformed military police are responsible for preventive policing and public order, plainclothes civil police investigate crimes, and federal police are responsible for interstate and international criminal activity. The largest force is the military police who, in their front-line role on city streets, are both the most abusive and most abused. But all these institutions—military, civil, and federal—are to some extent corrupt.

The chronic underfunding of Rio's police is well known, but it really hits home when we meet the straight-talking Inspector Marina Maggessi. Waiting for her in the lobby of a stuffy *delegacia*,* we watch the tired-looking duty officer tap out a statement on a battered typewriter. A typewriter? In Parada de Lucas, AfroReggae provides some of the city's poorest people with state-of-the-art computers and air conditioning.

Why the police are corrupt

Marina Maggessi: "You have a military policeman who earns 800 Reais a month and lives in a favela. His wife has to wash his uniform every day and dry it behind the fridge: No one can know he's a policeman. His kids can't be proud of him. They

---

* *delegacia*: civil police station

can't go to school and say that Papa is a policeman because, if they do, he'll be killed. When he gets on the bus he has to hide his ID in his shoe. He swallows his self-esteem because he's a piece of shit. He goes to the battalion and has to obey his superiors who have this military doctrine which adds up to *porra nenhuma*.* They tell him his shoes are dirty and that he'll be punished. So he goes out on duty, full of rage, and you can buy him for peanuts on the corner because anyone and everyone in the *sociedade bacana*† corrupts the police. And that's exactly why they get paid nothing—so they can be bought by others."

Abacate: "I don't blame the policeman who accepts a bribe. His salary is a *salário de fome*.‡ Traffickers earn a lot, so if a policeman catches a trafficker and gets some money out of him, I applaud that. It's wrong, but if he tries to survive on his paycheck he'll go hungry. He has to pay rent, transport, and he needs to look after his family. So the risk he'd take in arresting a trafficker isn't worth it. How do the authorities think they can fight drugs when their foot soldier is going hungry? I hate it when a policeman gets a *trabalhador* and beats him but, when he gets a trafficker—a guy who is earning thousands of Reais, I think what he should do is take the bribe and I'll shake hands with him for doing so."

Luiz Eduardo Soares: "Police corruption in Rio is a major problem. There are forty-five thousand professionals§ on the streets, military and civil. Of course they should act in cooperation but they don't. They have different cultures and func-

---

* *porra nenhuma*: fuck-all (slang)
† *sociedade bacana*: middle-classes (slang)
‡ *salário de fome*: hunger salary
§ approximately 35,000 military police and 10,000 civil police

tions that then work to deepen the differences they find at every level of their lives. So you have two organizations that don't talk to each other. Both of them are brutal and a great part of them corrupt. I can't tell you the exact number. No one knows the numbers engaged in corruption. We can't even say if it is the majority or not. But the fact is that those segments that are brutal and corrupt are really important, both in number and effect, because their action is substantial enough to undermine the police's image and the institution as a whole.

"There's an arrangement between corrupt police and criminals: 'You're not going to arrest or kidnap us, and we'll pay you a fee.' It's a kind of protection, a percentage of robberies or drug profits or even just a fixed amount. The arrangements vary, but for the police it's very simple: an outsourcing of risks and costs to the criminals. Nowadays, that's where we're at in almost every favela community.

"The organization of this is local and fragmented, but it's impossible not to see the corruption. If you visit the favela, you'll see it. And if you're a straight policeman, you just have to get on with your job because you know what might happen if you speak up. There are rare but consistent cases of police killing colleagues and, in some of those cases, the victims are people who've tried to resist the corruption."

Nourishing the monster

As the author of Lula's public security plan, Luiz Eduardo provides a clear insight into the links between government policy (both local and national), public attitudes, police corruption, and criminality. As an example, he talks about a gratification scheme (known as the "Wild West Bonus") offered by Rio authorities in the mid-1990s that promised a cash reward for police who killed alleged criminals. Removing any semblance of supervision or accountability, this policy effectively granted individual officers the power of life and death over anyone they designated a suspect. Implicitly, of course, it also gave officers the opportunity to sell this power—to kill or to spare for a negotiated price. Unsurprisingly, the policy proved to be an invitation to ever greater levels of corruption.

Of course, this initiative sounds ludicrous and self-evidently counterproductive. But you need to consider that it was backed by a public that demands tough measures to combat crime and tends to regard favela dwellers and criminals as one and the same. Consider, too, that it was introduced in a society whose dominant class has traditionally used the police to protect its own interests, and you can begin to see this initiative as a perpetuation of existing social mechanics. As Luiz Eduardo put it: "You are nourishing a monster in the police. And this monster becomes part of criminality."

Legally licensed to kill

> "*A partir que a polícia trabalha mais, mata mais.*"
> ("The harder police work, the more they kill.")
> — *Marcelo Itagiba, Rio Public Security Secretary*
> *in a meeting with Amnesty International, April 2005**

As well as receiving political, public, and media protection, police who kill in the line of duty also seem to be protected by the courts. Impunity is the norm. Take the military police colo-

---

* *They Come in Shooting: Policing Socially Excluded Communities.* Amnesty International, 2005.

nel in charge of the Carandirú prison massacre that happened in São Paulo in 1992. Riot police called in to quell an uprising killed 111 unarmed prisoners, most of them shot dead in their cells. No police were injured. In 2002, the colonel was tried in court and sentenced to 632 years in prison for his part in the operation. As he had no prior criminal record, he was free to appeal. While on bail he ran as a candidate in the state elections and now sits as a deputy in São Paulo's state assembly.

Another example: in 2003, official figures state that Rio's police killed 1,195 civilians. According to Luiz Eduardo, 70 percent of these killings bore the characteristics of executions, though nearly all were officially recorded as "resistance followed by death." This term, which has no recognized status in Brazilian law, automatically transforms the victim of a fatal shooting into an aggressor and ensures that very few fatal incidents are ever independently investigated.

The monster of the Baixada

BETRAYED TRAFFICKER WANTS TO KILL BEM-TE-VI'S WIDOW, ran the headline of O Dia on November 2, 2005. The head of trafficking in Complexo do Alemão is reported to want to kill his ex-girlfriend, who deserted him for his fallen enemy. Photos of the girl are splashed all over the front page: another day, another episode in the very public soap opera of Bem-Te-Vi's death.

Buried in the back pages of the newspaper we find some real news, a five-line snippet connected to the darkest episode yet in the history of Rio's police force: "Detective murdered in Nova Iguaçu. The chief inspector of the homicide department in the Baixada Fluminense, Marcelo Chaves Manoel, was shot dead in his car yesterday. He was fired at by attackers driving a silver vehicle. The policeman was taken to the hospital but died."

Quite why the newspaper chose to pay so little attention to

the murder is not clear. A couple of days later, another newspaper reports that the inspector was the victim of a robbery.
Perhaps. Perhaps not. His death, too, bore all the hallmarks of
an execution. So why would someone want to get rid of this
particular policeman? Maybe because he was in charge of an
investigation into the worst mass killing to occur in Rio since
the Vigário Geral massacre.

The Baixada Fluminense is an area made up of Rio's sprawling satellite municipalities, housing millions. Criminality in the
Baixada Fluminense is largely controlled by the infamous
"death squads"—groups of active and ex-police officers and
their allies. JB calls them *polícia mineira*,* a phrase used to
denote police who don't merely take bribes but are active criminal protagonists. Such groups typically run illegal private security companies, protection rackets, and drug sales. They
claim legitimacy with the local population by keeping the
streets clear of petty criminals, whom they execute in large
numbers. Who benefits from this situation? Those anthropologist Darcy Ribeiro describes as a *"lúmpen-burguesia de
microempresários*,"† small, locally owned businesses that pay
for "protection." It's in the Baixada that Luiz Eduardo's "monster" has been left to its own devices the longest.

On March 31, 2005, an armed gang, believed to have been
military police officers, drove unchallenged around several
neigborhoods in the Baixada for two and a half hours. They
killed twenty-nine people in eleven locations, including three
children and nine people in front of a single bar. Numerous

---

* *mineira*: literally "from Minas Gerais." In the 1960s and 1970s, Minas'
police had a particular reputation for corruption.

† *lúmpen-burguesia de microempresários*: lumpen-bourgeoisie of microbusi-
nesses

theories for the motive behind the massacre have been put forward. Some say it was a dispute between different factions within the police, or between the police and small-time drug dealers. Others suggest it was a reaction to recent attempts by the state government to clamp down on the activities of death squads. But no one really knows, and the investigating officer's been shot dead. Ten military police officers were arrested and charged for alleged participation in the attacks.

Informality and illegality

It's common for police officers to supplement their pitiful salaries by working in private-security firms. Many do so honestly. However, whether the individual officer is "honest" or not, many such firms are not legally registered. According to Luiz Eduardo, this leads to a blurring of the lines of legality, which creates conditions in which criminality can flourish. He explains it like this: "The state budget is made viable by this situation. If the [public security] secretary took a strong position against it, we'd have to pay the police proper salaries and the state budget would collapse. But if you just accept these private services, you have informality and therefore criminality. Why? It's obvious. Take the weapons they use in an informal private-security firm. Since the firm is informal, the arms can be informal, that is to say illegal. Of course you can be honest and try to use those weapons legitimately, but there will always be a few people selling arms to criminals and so forth because the state has no control over the situation. The line between informality and out-and-out illegality becomes very fine.

"When you're not in legal control of the situation, you're not in control of oceans of different practices, many of which are very dangerous. We know of policemen who will rob cars or even kill to sell private security to some neighborhoods. We have calm neighborhoods, safe neighborhoods, which will suddenly become very unsafe places because of exactly this practice. The policemen artificially create fear and then sell security. Often they'll make it very clear that, if people refuse to pay for private security, they'll have problems."

Reform?

Marina Maggessi: "The police need to stop being the ones expected to find solutions. In any place in the world, the police are the last state institution to enter an area. Here we're the only one. We work with the consequences, never the cause. It's like treating brain cancer with an aspirin to fight the pain, while all the time the cancer is growing."

There is a schizophrenia in Brazilian policing. On the one hand, a policeman is required to protect the rights of an individual; on the other, he is effectively expected to act as state executioner. He is a defender of the law even as his breaking it is implicitly condoned. In some circumstances he's indisputably powerful; in others he's "a piece of shit." In such circumstances, it's hardly surprising that the Belo Horizonte policeman can't look himself in the eye, or that the AfroReggae instructors believe that Rio, with its specific problems, is not ready for a cultural invasion.

Police reform has long been high on the political agenda, both at the state and national level. Luiz Eduardo knows this only too well. But he also knows why it is so difficult for any reforms to go further than the drawing board. In 1999 and 2000, he worked in the state Public Security Secretariat under Governor Anthony Garotinho. Garotinho initially supported efforts to fight police corruption. After just over a year, how-

ever, Luiz Eduardo was removed from his position, partly because the so-called *banda podre** began to exert internal
pressure against his plans and partly because Garotinho came
to realize that standing up for the reform of Rio's police was
no vote winner.

Three years later, Luiz Eduardo was in Brasília, occupying
the ministerial post of National Public Security Secretary in
Lula's new federal government. His highly thought-of plan,
which included detailed police reform proposals, had been fundamental to the PT's election campaign and, if implemented,
could have led to real change. But this time Luiz Eduardo lasted
only nine months before being replaced. The plan? "They kept
it in a drawer, and it's there, lying in a drawer, forgotten. In the
meantime, at state level, we're completely lost. There is no
policy at all. They're going into favelas in a warlike manner,
like terrorists, day after day. You kill one Bem-Te-Vi and there'll
always be another. At the same time innocent people are being
killed, suspects are being killed, and nothing changes. Corruption grows, brutality grows, and politics carries on as usual."

Against such a bleak backdrop, AfroReggae is taking quite
a risk entering the fray. Then again, taking risks is what they
do. Through culture they aim to transform the outlook and
mind-set of individual officers; it's exactly the same model
they've used for more than a decade working with favela youth.
They also aim to challenge the way society, especially young
people, views the police. So far, so good. The Minas project has
been a huge success. For most of the police officers involved,
it's the first time that any attention has been paid to their individual well-being. The police percussion band formed during

---

* *banda podre*: rotten bunch

the project has played onstage with AfroReggae and on national TV. A documentary called *Polícia Mineira** has followed the whole process. In December 2005, it was shown at an exclusive gathering that drew together Rio's highest-ranking police officers and members of AfroReggae. JB was there. He says it was very well-received.

---

* This time meaning "police from Minas" in the literal sense.

14

Three Survivors' Stories

We drive with JB from Vigário Geral to the AfroReggae *núcleo* in Cantagalo, high above Ipanema and Copacabana. It's late afternoon and the steep, narrow street is teeming with schoolchildren and people coming home from work, all trudging up the hill from the *asfalto*. AfroReggae's base is in the João Goulart-CIEP, a community center that's at the top of and yet slightly set away from the favela. It's quite a building. It was constructed as a casino (there's even an elevator that runs down to the *asfalto* throughout the day) but the owners were never granted a license, so now it houses various local projects, including AfroReggae's circus troupes (Afro Circo and Trupe Levantando a Lona).* Even on a gloomy day like today it boasts wonderful views over the favela to the beach and, on the other side, all the way across Lagoa to Vidigal.

Adriano has accompanied us from Vigário. He's a former *traficante* who's recently joined AfroReggae. Twenty-eight years old, tall, and well-dressed, he has a relaxed and confident man-

---

* Afro Circo is AfroReggae's professional troupe; Trupe Levantando a Lona (the Raising the Big Top Troupe) is the junior troupe made up of circus students.

ner. JB's teasing him about his umbrella, accusing him of being "a fairy." Adriano takes no notice.

As we're getting out of the car, we ask him how long he spent in the *movimento*. He lifts a finger to his lips and nods at a policeman sitting in a *guarita** a few yards away.

Inside the *núcleo*, the AfroReggae band is rehearsing but three of them—Anderson, the vocalist, and percussionists Dada and Altair—take time out to talk. These three are currently mentoring recent ex-traffickers who are now working with AfroReggae. Anderson takes responsibility for Adriano, Dada for BT, and Altair for Andre. Anderson calls it an "orientation process." This is "each one, teach one" at its most literal.

Sitting in a circle in a back room, Anderson sets the agenda. He speaks quietly but with eloquence and complete conviction. "In the community, the closest thing there is to structure is the traffic. So if you want money, power, women, or respect, the simplest way to obtain these things is the *movimento*. You don't see successful black people on TV or any images that could boost your self-esteem, so the closest thing you have to look to is the traffic and you see that every day. In a way, Afro-Reggae consciously mimics the organization of the traffic—our clothes, our structure, even our slang—because we want to mirror what attracts young people. But, of course, we try to show that you can make money and attain power through other means—through your creative abilities.

"Here we are sitting with three different individuals who went into trafficking for three different reasons. For Andre it was because he lost family members and any sense of hope, for BT it was fear of the police, and for Adriano it was an economic decision. These are all factors that push people

---

* *guarita*: sentry box

into o *tráfico*. And of course there are other reasons, too. Some people want power, others simply want to be in a position where their decision-making actually matters, others just want to be in a structured network of friends. There are many reasons."

Anderson sits back and we start to talk. Certainly the three former *traficantes* could scarcely be more different from one another in terms of appearance, attitude, and personality. Adriano is lanky and cocksure and seems mildly bored. BT is short, muscular, and eager to please with his face wearing a permanent grin. Andre is diffident. He speaks slowly and deliberately, his brow furrowed in intense concentration.

The conversation takes a while to warm up. At first everyone seems a little nervous and edgy. Perhaps this is because the former *traficantes* have none of the band members' savvy when it comes to talking to gringos; perhaps the group is too large (it feels as strenuously confessional as an Alcoholics Anonymous meeting); or perhaps it's just plain embarrassing. It's only when Anderson, Dada, and Altair return to their rehearsal that the atmosphere seems to relax.

We all pull our chairs in closer, and now the anecdotes, jokes, and chatter fly thick and fast. Then Adriano says, "If we were all working in o *tráfico* right now and sitting round like this, one of us could be about to die. All the others would know who it was and who was going to kill him." He stands up and begins to prowl behind us around the circle. "We'd be sitting around talking, one of us might be cleaning his gun, and then it would be 'Pow!' And that's it."

Adriano has just shot Damian through the back of the head with his index finger. BT and Andre are nodding their agreement and adding details. We plan more talks with these three over the next few days.

Andre

"I was in and out of jail for about two years between 2001 and 2003. When I got out, I spent six months outside the faction. I looked for work, for other possibilities, but it was very difficult and I got involved in the *movimento* again. Basically, at this time, my life was already over. My father was dead, three brothers had been killed in *o tráfico,* and I only had my mother at home.

"I already knew Junior and we did have some kind of dialogue. He put pressure on me. He used to say, 'Look, you're not getting anything out of this. You've already lost three brothers to this lifestyle and the only thing you can see in your future is more loss. You'd better just get out.'

"But I was doubtful. I thought, 'This is my life; it's what I do.'

"Then, one day, I was out with my rifle on the corner and the sun was beating down. I looked up at the sky and did some soul-searching. I bowed my head, said a prayer, and asked God to help me get out, but to help me get out in a clean way that meant I didn't owe anything and I didn't have to worry.

"Three days passed and I got in a fight with another guy in the faction. I just didn't like his attitude. Both of us were banned from the *boca* as punishment. When the punishment was over, I came back and talked to the *gerente geral* and told him, 'I really can't do this anymore. I need to do something else.' And I left.

"For two months, I didn't do anything. But then my stepfather found me a job at a bus company. I got my work card signed and I was ready to start within a week. But then something happened.

"My stepfather and I got on the bus to go to the bus station. There were two guys sitting up front and they definitely had some kind of plan. One of them was talking to the driver and the other was staring at me really badly. So my stepfather said, 'Let's go and sit at the back.'

"Unfortunately, at the back was another guy and a girl, and they were clearly in on it. They started walking up the bus. The girl had a leather bag with a gun inside. Then the driver slowed down and began to pull toward the curb. Clearly that's what he'd been told to do. My stepfather grabbed me and shoved me off the bus because it was obvious they were about to kill me. I looked back and they were watching me. They made a signal: 'Next time you're dead.'

"I don't know who they were. They must have been from another faction. That's one thing about being involved in *o tráfico*—you may not know a lot of people, but a lot of people know you.

"When we got home, I told my stepfather I couldn't take the job. I'm not a cat and I've only got one life. It was too risky.

"My mother was really supportive. She said, 'OK. We'll help you out until you can find another job.'

"But my stepfather was putting me under pressure, saying, 'He doesn't want to do anything with his life; just hang around the favela and waste time.'

"Basically I was stuck at home again. So I got back into the game.

"This was Christmas last year. My first job was taking care of the arms stock. At five in the morning, I'd pick up the rifles from the traffickers and store them. At three in the afternoon, I'd take them back out. That was my routine and I got paid 100 Reais a week.* I only did this for about three weeks before I

---

* Calculating the real value of traffickers' wages can be difficult; partly because they vary from *favela* to *favela*, partly because they've fallen significantly over the last few years, and partly because the value of the Brazilian currency has also fallen. Anderson, for example, told us that, seven or eight years ago, a job like the one described by Andre would have paid as much as 1,000 Reais a week, at a time when one Real was worth one U.S .dollar (it's now more than two Reais to the dollar).

was transferred to Caxias. There, I was managing three *bocas* and it was much better paid.

"But during this whole time, I still wanted to get out. Then JB came and took me into AfroReggae. Junior was waiting. He said, 'If I could give you a position here for five hundred Reais a month, would you leave this life that you're leading?'

"I was, like, 'Man, I'd leave this life just for different work, not because of the money.'

"Right there on the spot, I was contracted by Junior and I asked for a week's leeway to get out of the traffic.

"During this week, I found myself trapped in a situation where I was completely surrounded by the police. I was jumping from rooftop to rooftop to get away. Then I got into this house and locked the door. It was a really weak door and you could have kicked it in, no problem. I thought I was finished. I was about to be another statistic. I started praying to God to help me get out of this situation. The radio was on in the house and it was playing a church hymn. I thought about turning the radio down but I decided not to. I got on the phone and called my friends and family to let them know where I was. I had a wash, lay down on the bed, and waited.

"The cops were searching everywhere. They went into the house next door. I could hear them shouting, 'When we catch him we're going to rip his head off and play football with it!' At one point, they must have been no more than a couple of meters away. But they never came into the house.

"I had nothing to defend myself with, so this was a moment of terror and despair. I reflected a lot and made myself some promises. At one point I thought about making a run for it, but I saw a man across the street who looked up at me and made a signal with his eyes: 'Be careful, the police are still around.' I was in that house for about four hours before they finally gave up.

"The following Saturday I left the traffic. I went back to AfroReggae and Junior put me to work with Altair. Without this opportunity, I could have been dead.

"When I joined AfroReggae, I started writing a journal so that I can pass it on to the younger generation and show them what it was like in the traffic. A lot of youth here, particularly those between eleven and thirteen, are very seduced by it, so I want to show them the reality, for good and bad.

"When you get into o tráfico, you don't have the right mind-set but you know that if you're naive, you'll die. So, if you're smart, you listen and observe—listen more, talk less. It's a kind of brainwashing.

"I had a friend in jail who really looked out for me. He taught me many things, including how to be a good trafficker. I learned from him humility, simplicity, purity, to honor your name at any cost and to honor the name of the Comando Vermelho. He also taught me that it's not about what the trafficker says but something he shows in his behavior. He's part of the community and must be respectful, never arrogant.

"Is this guy happy I left? Of course he is. But he's still in it. And that hurts because I know he's got a good soul. It's hard for him to get out, let alone get a real job, because of his seniority within the movimento. In the life that he lives, he can't leave the community. He can't take his kids for a walk because it's too dangerous. If the cops see him, they'll shoot him.

"If you've been good at your job, the faction won't give you problems when you leave. But trying to start a life as an honest worker is difficult. It's almost impossible to find an opportunity, but also your head is scarred. One reason people return to trafficking is because they can't get used to the outside world. In the traffic, you lose your vision of what's going on outside the community. You're not connected to any other world, only to the life inside. That's why I say that leaving *o tráfico* has to be like a second brainwashing.

"I don't have the anger that I used to. I had to get out because my mom suffered when I was in jail and she's already lost three sons to the traffic. So now I live my life in a tranquil manner and I won't stress about anything. I don't ever want to go through that lifestyle again. I just put everything in God's hands."

BT

"I only became involved in the *movimento* in January this year. It's different for me because I wasn't raised in the favela. I came from the *asfalto* and I'd already had a real job. I was in the army and then, when I left, I worked at a fast-food joint: midnight to six a.m., six days a week. Then I worked for a plastics company—steady work. It's a crazy thing because one day I was working nine to five in a regular job, and the next I'm a trafficker, walking around the community with a gun in my hand.

"The thing was, I enjoyed going to the *baile funk* in Vigário and it wasn't long before the police knew my face. They started to point me out and, when I walked past, they'd make me a target: 'Look! That's the guy who likes to hang out in the favela!'

"Then I heard that a police officer was looking for me. I was one of the people on a list, and he was crossing off names, deciding who was going to be punished and who was going to die. One time, I happened to be walking past his car and I looked in and I saw my name on that list. Another time, he actually came to the company where I was working and asked for me, but luckily I wasn't in the building. As it turned out, this cop was one of those involved in the massacre in 1993. I figured that, if the police were going to kill me for being a trafficker, I might as well become one.

"I took all my clothes, moved to the favela, and pretty much forgot about my life in the *asfalto*. After a while, my mother called me and said, 'Where are you?'

"I told her, 'I'm in the community, I've got a rifle in my hand, I'm at the *boca,* and I'm working.'

"She started crying. She said she was going to take me away, send me to Minas Gerais or São Paulo.

"I started off as a *gerente*. What separates the good trafficker from the bad? I don't know. But I didn't sniff coke or smoke weed, and that was a good point because there was no risk factor. We dealt a lot with guns. Not everyone knows how to take a rifle apart, but I'd been in the army. After I came into the favela, I learned how to pick apart other kinds of weapons, too.

"But mostly a good trafficker displays a 'disposition.' For example, there's four of us on duty when the guys from Lucas invade. Two run away because they're scared, but we stay and get in a shoot-out. That's a quality that shows we're worthy and we'll move up in the ranks and become known.

"Soon after I joined, Andre left the traffic but I stayed a while longer. Later, after he'd joined AfroReggae, he'd pass by and say, 'Don't you want to leave this lifestyle? If you don't get out, you'll end up dead.' That's when I decided I wanted to join AfroReggae, too.

"On Father's Day, I had a big shoot-out with the TC, and

the following Monday I left the traffic. Andre asked about me at the *boca* because he knew about the shoot-out and he hadn't seen me for a couple of days. But the guys were, like, 'He's fine. He quit the traffic and he's at home.'

"So Andre came to see me and we chatted. He told me that he couldn't guarantee me a position in AfroReggae but he'd see what he could do. I got out of the traffic on August 15 and started working with Dada.

"*O tráfico*? I know it's shit, but I still miss it. People say that the trafficker can't make real friends because he's in this way of life. But I definitely made real friends and I'm sad because not many have the opportunity to get out alive and start again.

"I don't think the traffic taught me anything other than survival. Before I was in it, I worked for a company and had to respect the rules or I'd be fired. In the CV, there are commandments and, if you go against them, you're killed. I didn't learn anything good. I just learned that if someone messed up and the boss said you had to kill him, you had to kill him. There were only bad things.

"If I hadn't found AfroReggae, I'd be dead. One day, when I grow up and have kids, my only concern is that they never go through what I went through in the *movimento*. AfroReggae is a different kind of work, but it offers a future. In trafficking, there's only the present. All you get is women, guns, respect, jail, and death.

"AfroReggae teaches me that I won't better my life unless I really want to. I'm very grateful. Everybody deserves an opportunity but most young people don't have the chance to join so I know they're pinning their hopes on me.

"I had shoot-outs with the cops and the TC, but they never saw my face, so they don't know who I am. The only people who know me are in the neighborhood where I lived. Sometimes I'm kind of scared to walk around on my own because they know what I did.

"When I got out and joined AfroReggae, I left the favela for the first time in months. I called my mother and went to this music shop near where my father has his business. That's how I got to see them again. Dada went along with me to guarantee my safety."

Adriano

"I got into drug trafficking in 1997. Until then I'd been in another state playing football for six years. I came back to Rio because I'd argued with someone and quit. I'd never been involved in crime before but had connections through my family. When I got back, my mother had nowhere to live and we stayed with an aunt. It was awful living like that.

"Not long afterward I started working for a cousin as a *fogueteiro*. At twenty I might have been old to start in that position but I wasn't really bothered. I earned 150 Reais a week. After a month, there was a shoot-out with the police. A friend got hit and his gun fell so I picked it up and fired some shots. Then I began to work as a *vapor* selling *maconha* and *pô** and began to earn more money. It turned out that I was good at accounting. There was never any money missing in return for the stuff I was given to sell. I did that for a few months and was able to get my mother a place to live. It wasn't long before I was a *gerente*. Why was I good? I was reliable. If you're good at your job and trusted by those in charge, you'll go up. Anyone in positions above you makes a mistake and you'll be promoted to take their place. It's like climbing a ladder. The funny thing is that when you get to the top is when you've had enough.

---

* *pô*: literally "powder," one of many terms for "cocaine"

"I don't even think about going back to that life. I once lost a whole gang in front of my eyes. I don't know why I didn't die, but for some reason they didn't shoot me. I was just sitting there with my gun, completely clueless. An order had come from within the faction saying we had to be killed. Eight people died, including my then boss. Another time I saw someone cut in half while he was still alive. The two pieces of his body were dumped in a can and set on fire. It's a very dark business. I never got involved in that sort of violence, but you end up working alongside guys who like it. They do it to get a reputation and in trafficking that's the type of person you come across most. I was lucky and never got sent to prison even though I was picked up by the police loads of times. Once I was handcuffed to a wooden lamppost in the street. They started by beating me on the soles of my feet, then they gave me electric shocks.

"At the point I left *o tráfico* I was in charge of the favela along with someone else. This guy had a certain way of operating. He liked to kill and beat people up. I only ever did what was necessary. All the *moradores* used to come to me with their problems. They were scared of him because he was too arrogant. He was a terrorist, a real Bin Laden character. All the work was left to me. I looked after the guns, wrapped the drugs, and kept the accounts. At the end I was stressed and overworked so I packed it in.

"The people living in the community must be treated well. You want them to respect you, because you rely on them. The resident can live without the criminal, but the criminal can't live without the resident. If Vigário Geral were populated by criminals alone, what would the police do? Come by, chuck a bomb in, and blow the whole place up. Traffickers depend on the community. Anyone who says they don't is the biggest liar in the world. The *morador* is the heart of the favela.

"There are two sides to the mind, I don't know if you've perceived this. One side can think right, the other wrong. I don't know if that's how it works with you but that's how it is with us. Just the other day, a guy came to see me saying that he had an easy robbery and he wanted me in on it. Although I said no, part of me thought, 'Go on, just do it, it'll be over quickly.' But I'm immunized now. I won't go back to crime.

"Nowadays I work as an adviser for Anderson. I'll act on his behalf, run jobs for him, and do whatever there is that needs to be done. I'm a sort of assistant. I like it because it's not the sort of job that suffocates you. Obviously you have your tasks to get on with, but there's not that constant pressure that you suffer in some jobs. So you can breathe. AfroReggae doesn't pull people out of traffic; it orients them. The person will only get out if they want to. What AfroReggae does is help find a way. They might show you a computer and teach you how to type. For someone who only understands crime, just messing around with a computer is a new beginning in itself.

"What if my five-year-old son thought of going into trafficking one day? I refuse to think about it. As a parent I'll try to give him everything I can, not just everything he wants, because I think that children need to be brought up with both hardship and freedom, so they can distinguish between right and wrong. If he wants to be a doctor, I'll try to help him. The thing that we need most urgently in Vigário is a school, a decent one. At the moment the nearest secondary school is a bus ride away. If there was an education center here for adults I'd be studying. In fact, whatever happens, I'm going back to school and AfroReggae is helping to find a place where I can study."

Survivors indeed

Andre, BT, and Adriano are, of course, the lucky ones. Afro-Reggae doesn't have the resources to reach everybody and, besides, their methods can't hope to suit every individual. Participation in their projects requires strict personal discipline and, though uncommon, it's far from unknown for disputes to arise and young people to drop out and join or rejoin o *tráfico*. AfroReggae has invested heavily in these three, and their future looks promising. The alternatives are miserable.

In December 2005, less than a month after these conversations took place, a single military police *caveirão* drove into Vigário, the favela where Andre, BT, and Adriano all worked. It was three a.m. Seeing it was the police, the *soldados* on duty opened fire, at which point the vehicle sped off in the direction of Parada de Lucas. The traffickers pulled back, taking refuge in a house together.

Shortly afterward, the *caveirão* returned and stopped outside their hiding place. Trapped inside, the traffickers gave themselves up to, as they believed, the police. It was the police, and then again it wasn't. From the *caveirão*, alongside some genuine officers, several traffickers from Lucas emerged dressed in police uniforms. They searched other houses and picked up a total of ten men before driving back toward their own community.

It is worth pointing out that this *caveirão* came from the same battalion that had been paid 200,000 Reais by the Terceiro Comando not to intervene during the 2004 invasion.

Two of the men abducted from Vigário that night were identified as *trabalhadores* by their captors and subsequently released. The remaining eight, identified as traffickers, have "disappeared" and are presumed dead. Despite the public outcry, media attention, and intervention of both the state public security secretary and the human rights secretary, a full-scale occupation and search of Lucas has failed to find any trace of those abducted.

15

Trabalhadores or Traficantes

"I am an invisible man . . . I am a man of substance, of flesh and bone, fiber and liquids—and I might even be said to possess a mind. I am invisible, understand, simply because people refuse to see me."

—*Ralph Ellison*, Invisible Man

Last amongst equals

Talk to Junior enough and you'll find that, above the grass-roots of AfroReggae's work—using culture both to extract young people from *o tráfico* and to keep them away from it—he keeps returning to twin concerns. These are to raise the self-esteem and the aspirations of favela residents and to change the attitude of wider society to favela communities. They are worthy aims and echoed by everyone from Luiz Eduardo to Denise from the Ford Foundation.

But they might lead you to a mistaken conclusion, which must be dispelled right now. They might lead you to think that every citizen in Rio is equal and that those in the favelas are simply unfortunate to live in neighborhoods that are occupied by an army of drug traffickers. Nothing could be further from the truth.

What follows must be a statement of the obvious to readers of this book so far, but there's no harm in spelling it out again: *favelados* are not equal with other citizens but systematically excluded—historically, financially, legally, and racially—from wider society.

Favela state of mind

One consequence of this exclusion is that the interaction between the residents and *o tráfico* is not one of civilian population and occupying force but a highly complex and nuanced relationship that can be difficult for an outsider to grasp.

There is a hip-hop track by American rapper Nas called "New York State of Mind."[*] In it, he details his experiences and aspirations growing up in the low-income Queensbridge Projects and the criminal psychology fostered in such an environment.

There is also, undoubtedly, a "favela state of mind." It's not explicitly criminal, but its interaction with criminality is ambiguous. If you live in a community beyond the rule of law, what constitutes illegality? While the vast majority of residents don't see *o tráfico* as "a good thing" and would certainly not want one of their family to join, they do recognize its temptations and are inevitably immersed in its culture.

At the most basic level, every resident knows somebody who's directly involved in the traffic. The statistics make that unavoidable. But more subtly, every resident is more or less in thrall to the traffic, too.

As ever, it's worth hearing what JB has to say about this. In one conversation with a couple of ex-traffickers, we started to discuss the rules of the Comando Vermelho. But JB was more keen to explain the way rules applied to the whole community.

---

[*] Nas, *Illmatic* (LP). Columbia, 1994.

"It's not 'the Ten Commandments,'" he said. "It's more like a thousand commandments, and you only learn them by living in the favela. They are unwritten, unspoken law. But when you live here, they become part of your thinking."

So what is this way of thinking and how does it work in practice? Here are three examples that touch upon different aspects of this state of mind.

First, the factions monitor movement in and out of each community. For a favela resident, a young person most of all, your psycho-geography is mapped through your membership of a community controlled by whichever faction. Day to day, therefore, if you need to cross the city, the best route is not as the crow flies, nor that served by a bus; rather, it is the route that ensures you never pass too close to "enemy territory." This may sound straightforward, if enormously inconvenient. But think about it a little more deeply and you realize that it actually requires an awareness that permeates your every choice. There is, for instance, a public swimming pool in Ramos, close to the Complexo do Alemão, right on the front line between the Comando Vermelho and the Terceiro Comando. If you want to visit this pool, what color swimsuit will you wear? To ensure your neutrality, you'd be well advised to avoid CV red.

Second, in the absence of any meaningful state presence in the favela, the *movimento* is generally the closest thing to local government. It is the faction that resolves disputes and punishes crime but it also often provides civil facilities. They put on the *baile funk*, of course, and they may build amenities that benefit the whole community—even Robertinho de Lucas's notorious "water park" is not unique. November 2005 saw Rio's newspapers feature aerial photographs of an illegally built, faction-financed swimming pool in a favela called Dendê.

However, it is at the individual level that the all-pervasive nature of the factions' presence becomes most obvious. If a family member falls ill and requires expensive medical care, to whom can the average resident turn but the traffickers? It is in these small transactions that webs of gratitude and obligation begin to be spun. Indeed, it is typical in many different favelas to hear the *dono* sincerely described as "a good man" who "helps the community" or "keeps the community safe."

Third, it's worth noting that it's not uncommon to find that residents describe those from rival communities as *alemão*; not just the *traficantes* who control that community, but its residents, too. They are "the enemy." Initially, this can seem absurd, since the residents of each favela lead almost identical lives and face the exact same problems and privations. But again, a moment's thought makes the judgments all too explicable. If you're raised to distrust your neighbor and he lives in a community you'll never be able to visit, and your only experience of this community is when its *soldados* are shooting, apparently indiscriminately, at you and yours, this hostility is the inevitable consequence. Nowhere is this more apparent than in the conflict between Vigário Geral and Parada de Lucas described previously. Unsurprisingly, it's not rare to hear rumors circulating that detail atrocities committed in rival favelas; no thought is given to equivalent rumors that are undoubtedly making the rounds just across the front line.

There is a depressing irony in these judgments, since one of the biggest problems facing favela communities—one that AfroReggae continually tries to combat—is the conflation of *favelados* with *o tráfico* by the media, the "city proper," and the police. But the truth is that when some *favelados* consider the residents of a rival favela, they are guilty of the very same conflation. It's a sobering example of the perniciousness of this mind-set.

The invisible

If favela residents' relationship with *o tráfico* is complex, their relationship with the police is anything but. If they typically regard *o tráfico* with more or less resentful resignation, they typically regard the police with little short of disgust. They may not trust the factions, but they trust the police a whole lot less, arguably, even, the state the police purport to represent. This is partly because faction rules forbid any interaction between the community and the police. As Leida put it, "It's difficult for the cops, too. The residents can't speak to the police, not even 'hi.' It's forbidden. If they say anything to us, even a respectful 'good day,' we have to put our heads down and go." It is mostly, however, because the overwhelming majority of *moradores* will have suffered at police hands at some time or another. In the worst-case scenario, this might mean an unprovoked beating or even an execution. But it is also a day-to-day reality of low-level abuse and exclusion.

We go to talk to Paulo Baia, the undersecretary for human rights in the state government. A respected academic (and professor at Rio's Federal University), he's a large, good-natured, and relaxed character. But listen to him for five minutes and you can't help but wonder if his laid-back demeanor is the inevitable result of years spent swimming against the tide. Much of what he says is depressingly familiar but it bears repeating, both for the specificity of his illustrations and, for a politician, the extraordinary straightforwardness of his perspective.

"Over the years the *favelado* has been transformed into a synonym for a criminal. This vision is reinforced by the Brazilian press, radio, and TV. Obviously this has a negative impact on the lives of the population who suffer violent and racist repression at the hands of the police. If the population in favelas is basically *mestiço* or *negro*, you already have a suspect.

The police attitude is that all *favelados* are criminals and, if not, they must be accomplices. Consequently, we are faced with a situation where two million people suffer various abuses every day—lack of transport, health, and education, as well as police oppression.

"Last week, for instance, the police put up barriers and blockades to stop people from the favelas from getting to the beaches by bus. In a completely arbitrary way they sent the buses back, saying they weren't registered and so forth. I have the following explanation: In the Zona Sul you have two hundred and fifty thousand residents and almost everything that is done in this city is done for them. The rest of the population is abandoned. It's a deliberate policy of 'containment': this is even the word used by the public security secretariat.

"The police have various ways of working: They might send the bus back or take the passengers off the bus telling them they are suspects and then leave them by the side of the road. The people lose their bus fares, but they're scared of the armed police, so that's that. It happens at any large event—football games, Carnival, New Year's Eve. It happens on the Avenida Brasil all the time. We receive many complaints and act immediately.

"Generally it works like this: Our opinion is that we should punish the commanders, but they never accept responsibility. The high command says it didn't order the action, so responsibility falls on the individual officer in the street. And who is he? Typically a poor black man himself."

It is precisely this kind of situation that sustains Rio's vicious circle of fear (for the *asfalto*), brutalization (for the police), and curtailed opportunity (for the favela): fear generates oppression generates alienation generates fear . . . and so it continues.

Considering the column inches devoted to drug trafficking, considering the way many favelas tower over the "city proper," it is frankly remarkable how little two-thirds of Rio's population typically know about the lives of the rest. This is not to say that all citizens are uncaring, wilfully ignorant people, but simply to point out that, over time, a status quo has been established that, at least superficially, benefits everyone but those with least hope of changing it—the *favelados*.

Walking out of our Copacabana penthouse, we occasionally hear gunfire from high above in the community of Tabajaras. We stop with other pedestrians and crane our necks curiously skyward, shading our eyes against the sun, but we can't spot anything. So we're left to wonder: What invisible man just shot that gun?

It's a half century since Ralph Ellison wrote *Invisible Man*; "invisible" is his description of black people's experience in racist America. It's only a few days since we were talking to Luiz Eduardo and, when he used the same word in his bleak assessment of the problems facing young people in the favelas, it certainly hit home.

"If you are a teenager, you are at a difficult point in your life in terms of identity-building. Who are you? What are your values? With whom do you identify? It's hard. But now let's add other components. Imagine you're black in Brazil, a racist society. Imagine you're poor in Brazil, an elitist and authoritarian society. What happens? People don't see you. They neglect your presence or even project a negative image onto you. And when you project a negative image onto someone, you're no longer seeing that person as an individual but simply the reflection of your own intolerance. And that experience of not being seen is very painful and destructive, especially for a teenager.

"So imagine you are young, black, and poor. You feel invisible and unaccepted. Then a trafficker gives you a gun, and it is the first time you experience life as an agent with a weapon. When you point that gun at someone, you produce a reaction in your victim and, in doing so, you become a person, you appear, you are visible.

"I'm not saying this is a good way of constructing yourself. Of course not. Rather, it's a desperate way of constructing yourself. But when you point the gun, you are holding it in your hand and that hand is claiming a relationship. You have the gun, which means aggression and violence, but you also have the hand that means a despairing claim for recognition and acceptance."

Choices

Go into any favela, ask a child what they want to be and, chances are, you'll hear one of two answers. Either they'll say they want to be a *trabalhador* (a worker) or they'll say they want to be a *bandido* (a criminal). If they say they want to be a worker, they're extremely unlikely to refer to a particular profession, let alone anything that might be construed as a career. Even from a young age, they recognize they'll be lucky to find any kind of poorly paid job. To be a worker means, more than anything else, to have a legal occupation and therefore demonstrable legal status that can be shown to authority. If, on the other hand, they say they want to be a criminal, they usually mean a trafficker. Even from a young age, they recognize that only *o tráfico* can offer them cash, status, and membership of an organization that gives them a very real identity as part of something bigger than themselves. As Luiz Eduardo put it, this is not a good way of constructing your identity but a desperate way. Nevertheless, functionally at least, it works.

When you ask children about their future, they're well

aware of their options: *trabalhador* or *traficante*. Their realism is frightening. And it's this realism, or rather this reality, that AfroReggae aims to change. At the very least, it offers a third option.

Back with Paulo, he explains his perception of AfroReggae's work; it is typically insightful. "AfroReggae is an example of a new social movement that works for the dignity and respect of the populations who live in favelas and want to stay there.

"AfroReggae is a paradigm. Why? Because it evolved at a very difficult time in Rio's history, in the aftermath of a police-sponsored massacre. Because they don't limit themselves to complaining. Because they are concerned not just about fighting the police but about bringing real change to the lives of people. Because they are not just a movement of volunteers but a permanent presence. Because they are not part of the academic or cultural elite. Because, with events such as Urban Connections, they create spaces that generate self-esteem for favela people who can then demand respect, both as human beings and as citizens."

Listening to Paulo speak with such candor, it's impossible to resist trying to elicit an overview of the city with what are, we assume, a couple of provocative questions:

Is the situation in Rio comparable with apartheid South Africa?

"There is a policy of segregation and programmed extermination of the poor population through social and ethnic targeting. Blacks and those of African descent, who make up the majority in favelas, are the principal victims. The difference is that in South Africa, apartheid was a legally sanctioned state of affairs. Here the apartheid was historically created. You have the marginalized populations, and the police act to contain these populations even though they should all be equal under Brazilian law."

So is it fair to talk about trafficking as a means of social control?

"I think so. That's true. That's my theory. I think that drug trafficking operates as a means of social control of these communities which favors the Brazilian elite. The groups of traffickers have no interest in changing the status quo and no interest in citizenship for the favelas. They are despots, deciding life and death for the population. And this is in the interest of the Rio elite. The city of Rio de Janeiro has a serious role in all this."

16

Junior

Moving to the city

"I was born in Ramos, a suburb of Rio de Janeiro, near the Complexo do Alemão and I went to live in downtown Rio when I was about ten years old. It was an important moment in my life, moving to the city, because I wasn't as streetwise as a ten-year-old from the suburbs would be nowadays. Things seem closer together now. Because of the highways and Metro, it takes a lot less time to get around. But when I moved to the city with my mother and two sisters, it was a big shock as I came face to face with prostitution, drug dealing, and illegal gambling for the first time.

"What really shocked me about seeing women selling themselves in front of my house is that some of them were mothers of friends of mine. My mom was a nurse, not a prostitute, so someone could call me "a son of a whore" and get away with it. But if someone's mother really was a prostitute, you could never say that.

"It was a very hostile environment but at the same time very rich. We're talking about the beginning of the 1980s. It was an environment in which the criminal was the hero. Back then the traffickers weren't the most famous bandits, it was the ones who ran the *jogo do bicho*.* There were a whole lot of gambling rackets. Of course, the guys who ran them didn't live in our area, because they were loaded. But as ours was a marginalized neighborhood, these things—the gambling, the drugs, the prostitution—they were our 'community facilities.'

"So when we moved downtown, I was innocent and the local kids really mocked me."

McDonald's

"When I was about twelve years old, McDonald's came to Brazil. Weeks went by and we heard those McDonald's songs on TV the whole time. It's more than twenty years ago, but I can still sing you the jingle. Naturally, we all wanted to go to McDonald's but just didn't have that kind of cash. So I started saving. Eventually I had enough to buy one Coke and one Big Mac, and I went to McDonald's with my friend Guilherme. Guilherme was a fat kid, really black.

"McDonald's was on Avenida Rio Branco, the main street downtown, and at that time of the weekend it was really deserted. When we walked in, we were completely overexcited. We ate our burgers as slowly as we could, drank our Cokes, and headed home.

"We took Rua Uruguaiana, which usually has a lot of trade going on but, being Saturday evening, was very quiet. We walked down the road banging on the shop shutters and stuff, messing around like kids do. Then one of the shutters set off an alarm and suddenly we found ourselves surrounded by the cops. We ran for it.

"I was pretty stupid at that time, but Guilherme was the

---

* *jogo do bicho*: the animal game. Brazil's illegal lottery bears many resemblances to the "numbers game" that once dominated urban slums in the United States.

same age and totally clued up. He'd been born in that area and had grown up among the criminals and prostitutes, not like me.

"The police started shooting. Guilherme kept going, running in zigzags and ducking, but I stopped in my tracks. The police caught me and started to beat me. By now, Guilherme was about four hundred meters off—he may have been fat, but he ran fast—but when he saw they had me, he came back.

"The police got nervous and started pointing their guns at him. The weapon used at the time was the twelve-gauge shotgun. But even so he still came back. They grabbed him and started to hit him, too. And he got beaten a whole lot worse than me because he was fat and black.

"When they finally let us go, I asked him, 'Why did you come back?'

"'Because I'm your friend.'

"I told him, 'I wouldn't have come back for you.'

"And he said, 'That's the difference between you and me.'

"From that moment on, I've always come back. Even now, if someone's in trouble, I have to come back. This point in my life was the doorway to my future.

"It's a great sadness for me that, in 1997, Guilherme died of AIDS and, even though AfroReggae already existed, I couldn't do anything to help him.

"Where I grew up, there was so much prostitution that a lot of my friends from that period have died of AIDS. Those who didn't die of AIDS are also dead. They died either because they were committing robberies or because they were with someone who was. I don't have a single friend from being a teenager. They're all gone.

"So in my adolescence, I grew up with lots of loss. And all

these losses were tied into drug trafficking, crime, and prostitution. It's for this reason that I never use drugs, tobacco or alcohol, because I saw so many people killing themselves.

"My father was an alcoholic, my mother smoked a lot of cigarettes, and my brother-in-law was addicted to cocaine. He injected cocaine, he didn't sniff it. There was even a period when I bought cocaine for him in the favela. That was my first experience of the favela, when I was twelve or thirteen years old, going in with friends to buy drugs for my brother-in-law, whichever community had the best gear.

"It was around this time that I began to marginalize myself even more. There were only two possibilities for me to gain status where I lived: either I could become a dealer or I'd have to become a good fighter. So I started boxing. At first it made me even more violent than I already was and I fought every day. I was up in court twice for fighting with police."

First victory

"When I turned eighteen, I achieved the highest grades in a test to join the army as a paratrooper. It was my first victory. Before this I'd only known losses so, for me, it was like being made the CEO of a multinational company. People changed their opinions. Just from hearing I'd done so well, I noticed that my neighbors saw me in a different light.

"One day I was talking to a friend of mine on our street. I already had this tattoo on my leg—it's a cross used as a symbol by Saudi Arabian soldiers to show they don't want to die—and I was sitting the way I am right now when three policemen walked past. They saw the tattoo.

"So this one cop—I even remember his name. He was called Louzada. I had shorts on and he started patting me down. It's one thing to search someone in trousers but I had shorts on and he was just slapping my legs. He took my ID papers, bundled them up, and threw them all on the ground.

"I had my certificate on me, the enlistment paper that said I'd passed the course and was approved to go into the army. As I said, this was my first victory and I was so proud. He ripped it up. I couldn't believe it.

"The other two policemen weren't doing anything, so I said to him as he walked away, 'So I'm going to have to pick this up?'

"He just looked back at me and laughed. I told him to go fuck himself. Back then I was a fighting machine.

"He came back. So I started slapping him right in the middle of the street, in front of everyone. The biggest humiliation is for a man to be slapped in the face, not punched.

"There was a metal name badge on his uniform, and I tore it off. I ripped his clothes and gave him such a smacking that he pulled out his nightstick. He tried to hit me, so I grabbed it and elbowed him in the face. He was getting beaten so badly I think he must have forgotten he had a gun and, for some reason, the other two cops did nothing.

"Finally, he started pulling his gun out but all the prostitutes came running. He couldn't shoot me because they formed a wall in front of me and I ran away. Unfortunately a squad car came by at this very second. Now they stopped me just because they'd seen me running, and that was it; I was arrested.

"The policeman who'd caused all the trouble turned up. He told them to take me to Sumaré, which is a place cops take people to kill them. We sat in the back of the car, another two officers in the front.

"I knew the way there, so I made a plan. We were driving really fast and I figured that, when we reached this particular bend, I'd kick the back of the driver's seat so that he'd jolt forward and the car would go over the edge.

"The guy next to me said again, 'Let's take him there and get rid of him.'

"And the corporal sitting in the front said, 'We're not taking him to Sumaré. I've seen his papers and he's been accepted as a paratrooper. He's not a criminal.'

"I told you these two stories—this one about the policeman and the one about Guilherme—and I could sit here and tell you others all afternoon. But these are the two stories that really marked my life. In the last twenty years, there have been lots of times that I almost died, but these were significant moments in forming and shaping my life."

Batman

"When I turned twenty-one I began to notice that, among young people in my area, I was the eldest. The majority of my friends were gone and the closest age group to mine was about fifteen or sixteen years old. So I came to be a kind of protector of this younger gang. It was about this time that I began to conceptualize AfroReggae.

"I started doing *funk* parties. *Funk* was already an illicit music at that point, but I've always been a *funkeiro*, ever since I was a kid. I'd do the *funk* parties but was also doing kids' parties, too, to earn money. I used to dress up as Batman because I was well-built.

"It's funny because where I grew up there were lots of homosexuals hanging around and it was common for this younger gang to have sex with them for cash. One day I was walking down the street. I was a pretty muscular young guy, and there was this man following me. He had the whole stereotypical homosexual manner about him. This bothered me.

"I'm calmer now, but I used to be a bit rough around the edges. So I turned around and said, 'What are you following me for?' I pushed him.

"He said, 'Hey! What did you do that for, *garotão*?'*

"So I thought he *must* be after me, and I started getting really pissed off.

"He said, 'I'm following you because I want to contract you.'

"I was just about to lose my temper. I said, 'Contract me? For what? You think I'm a prostitute?' I hit him.

"He put his hands up and said, 'What are you talking about? Calm down! I just want you to be Batman!'

"'What? Batman?!'

"'Yeah! I want you to do my kid's birthday party!'

"At this time I was at a very confused stage of my life. I'd given up on the idea of being a paratrooper and was super-unemployed. The only work I was doing was in a theatre. My friends thought I was becoming a little strange. They used to say, 'All this boxing? Acting? You're getting weird, man.' And then I became Batman.

"So what does it mean to be Batman? It means putting on a costume and charging into the party with as much energy as possible. Then you just jump around a lot and play with the kids and be hyperactive. I was Batman for two years. I've always had good relations with kids, and this proved it.

"So I was Batman by day and a *funk* promoter at night. Eventually I started making more money from the *funk* parties, but they were only for about a hundred people. It wasn't a big deal.

"When I was doing Batman, it was either at parties for kids of the super-rich in Leblon or Ipanema or at the opening of a new shop or something.

---

* *garotão*: big boy

"The last time I did Batman, I was on this big music truck with huge speakers. It was a promotion for one of the supermarkets, and we drove into a favela. On this truck was Superman, Spider-Man, Mickey Mouse, Pluto, Batgirl, Wonder Woman, and me, all dancing and singing. Spider-Man was the best, doing all this crazy climbing about. Then he decided to jump off the truck. I might have jumped with him, but my costume was the hottest and I was melting.

"The truck drove through the favela and all of a sudden we were, like, 'Where's Spidey?' We looked back down the street and all we could see was a little blue and red dot and dust kicking up. We shouted to the driver to slow down. Then we saw that the dust was thousands of kids running after him, throwing rocks, hitting him with sticks and shouting, 'Check out Spider-Man! He can really take a beating!' I tell you, the way he leaped back on the truck, he really *was* Spider-Man!

"The last show I did was part of the same promotion in another *favela*. Now, in the movies, Batman's outfit is bulletproof. So this kid came up to me holding a pistol and goes, 'Is your outfit *really* bullet-proof?' I stopped dancing around in my cape, got him in a headlock, kneed him in the face, took the pistol, and threw it away. I took off my costume and got the hell out of there. It's way too dangerous being a superhero.

"After that, I just did the *funk* parties and this was the first time that Vigário Geral and Parada de Lucas came into my life with the famous *arrastão* in Ipanema. At that moment, I wasn't the same kid who'd suffered so many losses. I started to feel differently. I was still throwing parties but I began to feel very spiritual and to investigate various religions. Then I discovered Hinduism and I developed a great love for Shiva, the god of destruction and reconstruction. And I began to learn about what it meant to be an entrepreneur."

17

A Different Way

"The potential value locked up in a house can be revealed and transformed into active capital in the same way that potential energy is identified in a mountain lake and then transformed into actual energy. . . . Capital is born by representing in writing—in a title, security, a contract and other such records—the most economically and socially useful qualities *about* the asset . . ."

—*Hernando de Soto*, The Mystery of Capital

Earlier in this book we wrote that AfroReggae is not a typical NGO. This wasn't a comment on other NGOs, just a statement of AfroReggae's uniqueness. In what has followed, many of the people to whom we've spoken have touched upon the key elements of AfroReggae's work and structure that set it apart. At this point, it's worth reiterating some of these elements to ensure that they're clearly understood, to explain some in a little more detail, and to allow us to touch briefly on the organization's future development.

AfroReggae's core purpose is both to remove young people from drug trafficking and to keep them out of it by providing other opportunities. These opportunities are made possible both by raising individual self-esteem and changing the attitude of wider society to favela culture. Such aims are entirely codependent since "exclusion" is something that infects, albeit often unnoticed, both the excluded and the excluding alike.

We have heard several times that AfroReggae consciously mimics the organization of the drug factions. Clearly this provides a familiar organizational hierarchy for former *traficantes*, but it also recognizes a "positive" role the factions can play in a young person's life. Put simply, in the frequent absence of social, educational, employment, or familial networks, the factions are often the closest thing a young person can find to a secure, structured environment. AfroReggae, therefore, offers exactly the same.

The next thing to say is that AfroReggae always wants to be seen and heard. Many of the experiences we've related and stories we've told have illustrated this, but perhaps we haven't expressed it as clearly as we might have done; it is, in fact, a more subtle point than is at first apparent.

We have described how, driving into Complexo do Alemão, for example, we could hear the sound of the percussion class from quite some distance; also how, in Vigário Geral, the kids in AfroReggae T-shirts are visible on every street. At one level, of course, this is no more than the nature of a percussion class or wearing a T-shirt as you would the colors of your favorite football team. At another level, however, it is a deliberate and ongoing attempt to reclaim physical and psychological space for AfroReggae's purposes, something that is fundamental when you live in communities beyond state control and the rule of law, communities that wider society tries to ignore. Implicitly, AfroReggae is always saying, "Look! You can see us. Listen! You can hear us. We're here!" And they're saying this nonstop to favela residents, the factions, police, politicians, media, and Brazilian society at large.

In any conversation with Junior, he will repeatedly come

back to the amount of media attention AfroReggae is able to generate. It's not a quest for fame for its own sake but part of exactly the same process. Every headline, CD, and concert says, "We're here!" In fact, they're at it again in this book.

What's more, AfroReggae is here to stay. Almost everyone we've spoken to—from Denise at the Ford Foundation to Luiz at Globo to JB—has made reference to the fact that, when AfroReggae enters a community, they're in it for the long haul. They establish a foothold in the neighborhood and become a part of its society (even if, as in Alemão, that takes two years to achieve). Again, this is not a comment on other projects but simply to point out that AfroReggae recognizes that changing the outlook and aspirations of socially and institutionally excluded young people is a lengthy process.

The last two aspects merit a little further examination. AfroReggae is not a one-size-fits-all program (or, as Junior and others like to say, "We are not McDonald's"). Different communities have different cultures with different problems that require different solutions.

Describing his initial entry into Vigário in 1993, Junior says the following: "I went into Vigário with a good advantage. My advantage was that I was so unprepared, so weak, and so unqualified. If I'd had wisdom and tried to lay my wisdom on the community, that could have been a problem because I'd have been imposing myself on them. Instead, my weakness became a positive aspect for my work, because I learned how to construct *with* the people."

What Junior says is undoubtedly both true and sincere, and one of the most remarkable features of AfroReggae's work is its genuinely inclusive, grassroots approach. But it doesn't tell the whole story. AfroReggae's projects are certainly constructed with the communities in which they work but they are also constructed pragmatically on the basis of realistic possibilities, available resources, and potential partnerships. Which leads neatly to the second aspect we would like to look at more closely . . .

Hang around AfroReggae long enough and it can be tempting to view the organization as the product of one man's drive and vision. Junior's name is raised in every conversation, be it with a politician or a former *soldado*, and he is at the hub of everything. Such a view is nonetheless somewhat illusory, and Junior himself is far too savvy to think in such a way. Of course AfroReggae's drive and vision is partly Junior's doing but it is also expressive of the relationships he's developed in all sectors of society, within the favelas and outside; with police and *traficantes*; with businessmen, politicians, and the media. As Junior says, "You can say 'I'm this' or 'I'm that,' but it's all bullshit. Without partnerships, you're nothing."

People, potential, and pragmatism

We head to Parada de Lucas on a miserable day in the pouring rain. JB pulls in on the Avenida Brasil and Evandro, the coordinator of the AfroReggae project in Lucas, meets us at the entrance to the favela. We skip puddles across the street to AfroReggae's *núcleo*, which is just 100 meters or so inside.

Although not quite finished, this is a hugely impressive, three-story structure. On the ground floor, there is a reception area, courtyard, and library; on the first floor, offices and computer rooms; on the top, a performance space where a capoeira class is currently taking place.

We sit down with Evandro and talk through the origins and development of AfroReggae's work here. Evandro is markedly different from the majority of the AfroReggae hierarchy we've met. While most of them are young, bustling enthusiasts, Evandro is a little older and more reserved. He's thirty-eight, a former systems analyst who was born and raised in Lucas.

"We've been active here since 2001, running computing classes. I found out about AfroReggae through seeing the band on TV. I didn't know anything about their social programs, but at the time I was unemployed, so it was just a job to me at first.

"It was the president of the residents' association who went to Junior and invited AfroReggae to come into the favela. Junior already had the idea of 'computer inclusion' classes and he had good contacts with a company that could provide us with the machines. At first, we had a three-by-five room in the Residents' Association building but, as soon as we started, it went crazy, with hundreds of people coming through the door. We soon realized that the community needed a better space, so we bought this building. At the time, it was only the basic structure, so we've had to create the whole interior.

"It was last year that we really got serious and started turning this into something. We founded other classes—like capoeira and comic book design. It began with the Parada Geral project, a cultural corridor between the two communities [Lucas and Vigário]. It was a great success, but eventually we had to stop the project because of the war. Nonetheless, it gave us impetus.

"Although our philosophy is the same, we have different objectives from Vigário. They intend to make musical bands, our projects are courses for individual development. We are a different community with different needs but also, because of the rivalry between the two favelas, we don't want to create any kind of competition.

"The work we do here is less visible than that in Vigário, and it can be a little slow. But we have a theatre group and an exhibition of comic books coming up. Besides, when this center opens properly, everything will really explode. It'll be a big evolution in the community, benefiting everyone."

A couple of days earlier, we had been to AfroReggae's *núcleo* in Cantagalo and talked to Carlos, the coordinator there. Like Evandro, he's a little older and his background is different again. Although Carlos was involved in the "implantation" of the Cantagalo *núcleo* almost a decade earlier, he was then working for the Brazilian National Circus School and he only recently joined AfroReggae full-time. Again, he talked through the origins and development of the organization's work in the favela.

"The circus was part of AfroReggae almost from the very start. Junior went to a convention in Canada in 1993 and met someone who was the director of the social programs of the Cirque du Soleil. He challenged Junior to create a circus project within AfroReggae.

"At first the idea was to make this happen in Vigário but Junior decided it was better to create the circus in a different community with a totally different reality. Then we had an invitation to start a project in this building and we knew that the same activities that worked in Vigário wouldn't work in Cantagalo, so that's why we tried the circus.

"It wasn't successful at first, and I'll tell you why. A much wider range of activities are available in Cantagalo than Vigário; there is already a samba school, capoeira classes, and so on. Also, here, we are in the middle of Zona Sul, so there is the beach just below us and other things young people like to do. So we were in competition from the start. But eventually, with this partnership with Cirque du Soleil, we had some artists come here—some Brazilian artists, too—and this started the dynamic of Afro Circo here in Cantagalo.

"We're going to have our ninth anniversary very soon, and we currently have more than 120 young people involved, mostly from Cantagalo but some from the *asfalto*. Last year, when I finished working at the National Circus School, Junior came to find me and he said, 'OK. You're going to come and work with me now.'"

Clearly, Carlos is yet another who's buckled under the weight of Junior's pointing finger!

Back in Lucas, after we've finished talking, Evandro takes us for a stroll around the community. We don't walk far and get the distinct impression that Evandro's not too comfortable venturing deep into the favela with a couple of gringos. It doesn't take long to realize that this is a very different neighborhood from Vigário in both atmosphere and look. It feels busier, better structured, more commercially vibrant. The buildings are more solid and there are more shops and businesses. There is a smelly canal that runs through the center of the favela, and if you narrow your eyes and look along its bank you could kid yourself you were in a rundown part of Naples.

When we think about it, Lucas is different from Vigário, but it's different from Cantagalo, Alemão, Vila Vintem, and every other favela we've visited, too. In fact, as we've already said, all the favelas are different. We have repeated time and again that wider Rio society frequently makes the mistake of equating favela life with criminality and the drug factions. But part of the reasoning in this equation is also to regard favelas as largely homogenous. The truth, however, also bears repeating: Favelas are very different from one another, arguably often more so than other neighborhoods, since they are such excluded (and therefore exclusive) communities. Relatively speaking, some favelas are rich and some are poor, some organized and some chaotic, some central and some suburban, and so forth.

In each of the favelas where AfroReggae works, therefore, the approach is unique. Their work is devised with the local population, certainly, but it is also devised with a clear view of what is possible and in association with the required personnel, whatever their background. In Lucas, the technology center is deliberately differentiated from AfroReggae's work in Vigário and is coordinated by a former systems analyst from within the community. In Cantagalo, the circus is differentiated from other available activities and coordinated by a professional from the National Circus School. AfroReggae has a consistent philosophy, but it's rooted in case-by-case pragmatism.

Capitalizing on capitalism

In his book *The Mystery of Capital** (subtitled "Why Capitalism Triumphs in the West and Fails Everywhere Else"), controversial Peruvian economist Hernando de Soto makes the following argument. Conventional wisdom, he says, suggests that developing nations are not historically and culturally attuned to entrepreneurship and, therefore, fail when it comes to capitalism. He claims that one glance at the vibrant entrepreneurial class in most developing countries should tell you that this is not true. Instead the truth is that in the West, thanks to formalized property rights, entrepreneurs are able to put their assets to

---

* Hernando de Soto, *The Mystery of Capital*, London: Bantam, 2000.

work as capital and collateral whereas, in the developing world (where such rights are at best more fluid), such capitalization is impossible.

Junior and his colleagues in AfroReggae certainly connect with the first part of de Soto's argument. At heart, they are not NGO workers at all but ambitious entrepreneurs. As for assets, we have already touched upon the illegality of favelas, so one might think that they conform to the second part of the argument, too. However, in the quotation with which we began this chapter, de Soto compared the potential value of a house with the potential energy of a mountain lake. AfroReggae may not have the house, but they do have the lake—it's a lake of favela talent upon which they intend to capitalize.

De Soto goes on to say, "Capital is born by representing in writing—in a title, security, a contract and other such records . . ." It is arguable that the most important written representations for AfroReggae's work are the numerous press articles they attract (in both local and international media) that allow them to develop a kind of "cultural asset base" that, in partnership with all sorts of business, can be turned into money.

Junior already travels nationally and internationally explaining AfroReggae's model to other NGOs and addressing businessmen about social responsibility. One day, sitting on his balcony, half-deafened by the church bells nearby, he tells the following story: "Two weeks ago, I was with a group of businessmen. One of them asked me how much I wanted for the AfroReggae band; how much I would sell it for so that he could exploit it for one year. I told him he would have to respect all the rules we have— like the band will not play at venues sponsored by alcohol or tobacco. And he offered me three million Reais.*

---

* Approximately $1.5 million at the time

"Obviously, I didn't sell. But just getting this proposal, my mind started to really tick over. I wasn't looking for such an offer. He came to me. But for a guy like this to offer me three million Reais for a year? I realized he'd want to make something like seventeen million Reais profit. I am not criticizing, but he's a businessman and he has no social feelings at all. What does he see in the band? Profit. So I'm going to do it without him."

In 2006, AfroReggae was restructured. To that point, it had two aspects: AfroReggae Artistic Productions Limited, a company that managed the profit-making sides of the organization (concert production, for example, and the work of the main band), sat beneath (and part financed) Grupo Cultural Afro-Reggae, the NGO, which runs the social programs.

Now a third strand has been added, called "Gas." Recent Brazilian legislation created a new kind of legal entity called an "OSCIP,"* which is basically an NGO that is able to generate profit and can bid to manage government-funded social programs. This is where "Gas" fits in. It has taken over the production side from AfroReggae Artistic Productions and also sells AfroReggae's services—workshops, lectures, consultancy—to government agencies and private businesses.

AfroReggae has grand plans which Junior articulates as follows: "The Ford Motor Company started a charitable foundation that supports us. We are a foundation that has now started a company. In 2004, we had a turnover of five million Reais. Of this we made one million directly, through sales of products, clothing, and party production. In 2005, we'll have generated thirty percent of our budget, with the rest coming from grants.

---

* *Organização de Sociedade Civil de Interesse Público*: civil organization in the public interest

Next year it will be even more. In five to ten years we'll be a hundred percent self-sustainable.

"There are two lines of thought. Either we can work like any other NGO, depending on continued outside funding, or we can create products of high artistic and cultural quality for commercial consumption and develop partnerships with companies, foundations, and government for mutual benefit."

"Partnerships": there's that word again. AfroReggae has no interest in holding out a begging bowl. Instead, they recognize that they have unusual products and skills on which they can capitalize in a commercial environment. In fact, they're already doing it.

Of the sixty projects AfroReggae runs, Junior estimates that 80 percent can also generate resources. Until now, for example, donor funding and the main band have bankrolled all of Afro-Reggae's subgroups (from the Afro Lata percussionists to the theatre troupe). In 2006, however, these sub-groups will be sponsored by the Brazilian oil giant, Petrobrás. Similarly, AfroReggae has done a deal worth almost three million Reais with Vale do Rio Doce, the world's largest producer of iron ore, which Junior explains like this: "We're going to have a partnership with them that has never happened before. I can show you a graph of the visibility of AfroReggae in the media and then you'll understand the interest of such companies. We are going to use their company logo in our projects and we will get around nine hours of TV coverage this year. If they paid for this coverage commercially, it would cost them more than 100 million Reais. We give them what they want, but we make sure the last word in any decision-making is ours."

Clearly, in such negotiations, AfroReggae is effectively leasing its cultural assets to major corporations. Doesn't Junior worry about the possibility of compromising their good name (one of their primary resources)? Of course he does, but his attitude is typically pragmatic.

"I don't accept money from alcohol or tobacco companies and I say no to a lot of people. I've also realized that when you are successful, you will always attract criticism. But Waly Salomão,* who was part of the inspiration for AfroReggae and my guru, taught me this: I don't have to answer for everything. Nike was accused of exploiting child labor in Asia, but you're wearing Nike shoes. Are you supposed to answer for that? You're sitting with me in my apartment. Am I not supposed to live in Zona Sul because of the work I do? Am I not supposed to talk to you because you're English and from an imperialist culture? That's stupid. I have to carry on in the real world. If I start raising the flag and saying I don't accept money from the English or the Americans or big business, I'll just be stuck in my ghetto and I won't speak to anyone.

"In the future, AfroReggae will be a social company. The focus of the company will be its social projects, but it will have the logic of quality and profit. At the same time, we will freely give the knowledge we have acquired to other social projects in Brazil and around the world.

"This is not about me. In some organizations when the leader falls, the organization dies. That will not happen to us because we have a structure in place. If I die, the organization will falter, that is natural, but it will come back stronger. There are two guys ready to take my place at any time: Altair and Anderson. Altair is a better administrator than me,

---

* Waly Salomão was a famous poet and a founder of the Tropicália movement.

Anderson has more charisma. AfroReggae will continue because we're on a road and there's no turning back. This is a capitalist world and we have to survive. Who knows? Maybe this is a quiet revolution, the revolution of the social capitalist movement."

18

The End of the Beginning

It's a couple of weeks since Junior told us the boss of trafficking in Vigário Geral wanted to get out and had requested his help. Today, Junior's going to meet him in the favela and he's asked if we'd like to tag along.

We drive to Vigário in an AfroReggae minibus and Junior's cracking jokes most of the way, relating stories of his spell playing Batman at children's parties. He's relaxed. He tells us that he hasn't been in Vigário for about two months because he's been busy giving talks around the country and with the main AfroReggae band for the São Paulo shows. "But I always know what's going on there," he says.

It's a bright Saturday afternoon. Vigário looks different in the sunshine. The streets are full of kids and the air thick with music and cooking smells. The whole neighborhood looks somehow more vibrant, more colorful, as if someone's given it a lick of paint since we were last here.

We meet up with Vitor, the coordinator of AfroReggae's *núcleo*, and stroll through the streets to the appointed meeting place. It's at Seu Jadir's house. The survivor of the 1993 massacre is now a respected elder in the community. We're shown inside.

We sit in a row on the one sofa. On the bed opposite, there's a small, motionless figure hidden beneath a blanket. We ask Junior who it is and he shrugs. It transpires it's Seu Jadir's frail and elderly mother-in-law.

The boss ambles in and perches himself on a small folding chair. He's a hefty character in a blue vest, denim shorts, and flip-flops. Junior had told us that he's younger than he looks but he surely can't be younger than forty. He manages to appear surly and yet somehow put upon at the same time.

The conversation takes no more than twenty minutes. Junior tells him he has no news. They're waiting on word from the Comando Vermelho *donos* in Bangu prison as to whether he'll be allowed to leave. Junior tells him it'll come any day now and asks him what he wants to do next.

"Anything."

Where does he want to go?

"Don't mind."

Junior tells him he can't stay in Rio because he has too many potential enemies and suggests a move to São Paulo. He says he can fix him up with a job and a place to live. The boss nods slowly. It seems like anything will do. He just wants out.

We all shake hands and head into the street. The boss turns left, we go right and walk up to the square by AfroReggae's temporary center, next to the pedestrian bridge that crosses the railway tracks out of the favela. We comment on the beautiful weather. Junior says it's because he's there.

AfroReggae has planned an *arrastão* for this afternoon and, in the square, the party's just warming up. There is a Red Bull–sponsored Hummer parked by the bar. It's customized to be a mobile sound system with an enormous speaker stack on the back and it's blasting hip-hop. It turns out that the music is by Marcelo De Gueto, who teaches AfroReggae's rap workshops and, every so often, the man himself gets onto the back of the vehicle, grabs a microphone, and delivers a verse or two. There are children everywhere: some dancing, some just watching in awe, others taking part in streetball classes on the court nearby.

At the bar, a few locals are enjoying a cold beer. Among them is Marcelo's girlfriend, who lives in the Zona Sul. She tells us she's never been to a favela before and if her mother knew she was here she'd go mad. But we remark on the brilliant atmosphere and how good it is to see kids playing safely in the neighborhood.

The comment is poorly timed. As if on cue, there's a series of loud cracks and everybody freezes. The music cuts. More cracks—definitely gunfire—and suddenly the crowd is scattering; adults running away from the railway bridge, kids throwing themselves on the ground behind the nearest walls. A member of AfroReggae shoves us up an alleyway in the cover of a building.

Looking up to the footbridge, we can see someone running across, then he disappears from sight. We think he's ducked and only later discover he's been shot. Bizarrely, we find ourselves standing next to an old lady in a Santa Claus hat. "*É Lucasss!*" she spits. "*É ooss alemão invadindo.*"

Soldados emerge from the favela shadows and start to fire apparently randomly across the railway. The shooting stops in less than a minute. The boss appears, carrying an enormous assault rifle. He looks the same—same vest, shorts, and flip-flops—but now he's very much the man in charge. He's so much bigger than any of his soldiers; then again, they're just kids. He climbs halfway up the footbridge, prowling. Vigário is his community, and he's defending it.

Gradually the story emerges. It transpires that police spotted a *traficante* on the wrong side of the tracks and opened fire. Running into the safety of the favela, he was hit in the leg. A woman has also been shot. She was just in the wrong place at the wrong time.

People are getting to their feet, dusting themselves off, and laughing. Junior has mistaken our shock for calmness and commends our bravery with a smile. The sound system starts up again and it seems louder than before. AfroReggae doesn't have guns, but they do have music. The *arrastão* continues. Sometimes just continuing is a victory in itself.

A few days later, we're at the launch of AfroReggae's album at the Circo Voador, an open-air venue in the Lapa District that's the heart of Rio nightlife. In the throng in front of the stage the atmosphere is buzzing but relaxed as everyone jostles forward for a better spot.

Walking around the outer fringes confirms what a diverse crowd this is, all ages and backgrounds. There are dozens of faces we recognize from AfroReggae's projects in all the different favelas. A guy from the residents' association in Alemão is sipping something cold; Evandro from Parada de Lucas is chatting to Patricia, one of the coordinators of Afro Circo in Cantagalo; and BT, the former *traficante*, greets us like long-lost friends. There are plenty of local celebrities, too, who will shortly be joining the band onstage—we can spot Brazilian rock stars O Rappa hovering in the wings while Caetano Veloso is mingling happily out front. Everyone's come out to support the local heroes in a safe space where they can freely mix.

The dimming lights silence the crowd as a voice over the sound system announces the band. Then, suddenly, the show's begun as a wave of sound rolls out across the audience before breaking over us where we're standing at the back. From our position we watch a ripple of arms as row after row throw their hands spontaneously skyward. Now vocalists Anderson, LG, and Dinho leap across the stage, punching the air, brandishing their microphones like weapons. And, for two hours at least, it feels like the whole city is theirs.

Damian's Story

Three years on

It's been three years since we wrote *Culture Is Our Weapon*. In that time, I have been working for AfroReggae in Rio, and the people Patrick and I interviewed in 2005 have become friends and colleagues. As coordinator of international relations, I have witnessed the organization's growth at home and abroad. There have been trips to China, India, Europe, and the USA; in Rio I have witnessed the inauguration of the Parada de Lucas nucleus in 2006 (attended by then Minister of Culture, Gilberto Gil) and a full opening for the nucleus in the Complexo do Alemão in 2007. This latter event was repeatedly postponed on account of months of gun battles between police and the Comando Vermelho that culminated in the largest single police operation ever seen in the city. More than 1,200 officers from various forces poured into the complex for one day—and killed nineteen alleged traffickers. I have not become blasé about the sound of gunfire, but I have gotten used to it. Just like motorcycles, dogs, *funk*, and firecrackers, it is an integral component of the favela soundtrack.

Culture Is Our Weapon ends with a shoot-out on the foot-bridge that leads into Vigário Geral. Over the last three years I have witnessed many others. Perhaps the strangest was at the end of a visit by African American students from a New York–based organization called the Brotherhood-SisterSol. These guys were traveling around Brazil on a leadership-building exercise, and I liked their serious demeanor: reserved and shy compared to their exuberant hosts. Their visit ended on a high, with an impromptu Brazil versus USA basketball game. We all laughed when one of the younger members of Afro Samba convinced a visitor to give him an I ♥ NY T-shirt; it hung to his knees like a dress.

I accompanied the group onto the footbridge with Anderson and Vitor. As we exchanged hugs and high-fives, I heard the same cracks that had rung out in 2005; except this time we were on top of the footbridge, sitting ducks. It was a tense couple of minutes before we had all fourteen Americans down the ramp and into the road on the other side of the tracks. In front of us, some five or six police officers had taken position beneath the footbridge, from where they fired a series of rounds into the favela. Vitor and I were last onto the minibus. A couple of the tough New Yorkers were lying on the floor behind the seats, terrified . . . and reasonably so.

On another occasion, I was with two percussionists from Bath, England. They had come to Brazil to brush up on their samba skills and play with the AfroReggae Carnival *bloco*. Waiting for a rehearsal late one Friday afternoon, we stopped on the corner opposite the footbridge to chat to Sandoval, the bar owner with a drooping mustache and heavy spectacles. As we sipped our Cokes, someone ran past—a kid with a huge stack of fireworks.

The firework of choice for raising the alarm is called a *doze em um*, and it makes a lot of noise: twelve rapid bangs, followed by one low boom. People scattered. The kid was lighting one fuse after another and the relaxed atmosphere had evaporated.

I spotted someone else running toward the footbridge. He turned his head and I realized he was grinning. In his left hand he was carrying an AK-47; with his right he gave me a thumbs-up. It was BT; back in the traffic. He said to me once: "I can't help it. I like it. It's what I do."

The adrenaline rush animated his face as he rushed forward to confront the police. Still gripping our Cokes, we ran behind him to take shelter in the nucleus. We learned that the *caveirão* had been spotted outside Vigário. Luckily, it turned out to be nothing more than a drive-by, and when things calmed down we headed back to the bar.

We found Sandoval grinning at us, his gold teeth—spades, diamonds, clubs, and hearts—glinting in the last of the sun. "You messed up," he said. "You ran across the line of fire. You must never do that." Sandoval has seen it all before, and he was more than happy to laugh at the panicking gringos; me included.

To live on the front line in Rio you have to hone your instincts, including the instinct to flee. Whatever the danger, you can't move on impulse alone: You must stay lucid and plot your escape route. If someone had shot at BT as we ran behind him, we'd have been exposed to the bullets.

The simple rule is to stay still until it's clear who's shooting and what they're aiming at; then you can plan your move out of the line of fire. This is one of the "thousand commandments" JB told us about, those unwritten rules that are programmed into the favela residents' conscious and unconscious, and that govern their every move.

Taking Over

There have been two significant developments in Rio since Patrick and I finished *Culture Is Our Weapon*. The first is the rise to power of the militias in the west of the city. These paramilitary groups with close ties to police and politicians are now said to control more than 150 communities. I discuss this in more detail below. The second is the successful invasion and occupation of Vigário Geral by the Terceiro Comando. After more than twenty years of hostilities, the Comando Vermelho was finally expelled from the favela in June 2007.

When news of this latter development emerged, I was with AfroReggae at a festival in Germany. We were told that Furica, the boss of Parada de Lucas, had simply walked into Vigário Geral with sixty soldiers early one morning and taken control. How was that possible? It was Altair who told me the story.

A couple of months before, Chico Rambo, the *dono* of Vigário Geral, was finally released from prison, where he'd been held since the early '90s. But instead of returning directly to Vigário, he holed up in Mangueira, another CV stronghold. Vigário, therefore, fell under the temporary command of a woman called Rose, who'd been brought in specifically to hold the fort. Although popular, she became frustrated when her repeated requests for more soldiers and weapons were ignored by the CV command structure, and eventually she pulled her team out, leaving the favela in the hands of a small group of young, poorly armed traffickers. When news of this reached Furica, he assembled a Terceiro Comando force and radioed ahead to Vigário—"We're coming in." Hardly a shot was fired as the remnants of the CV force realized they had no chance and slipped away.

Furica immediately sent a message to the AfroReggae coordination team. This was a peaceful invasion, he said, and there would be no repetition of the looting and confusion of 2004. Relatives of traffickers and people linked to the CV were given a short time to organize themselves and leave the favela. Vigário was now Terceiro turf.

The next few months saw two attempts by the CV to retake the community. The first included a day of gun battles during which witnesses reported seeing two police *caveirão* from different divisions shooting at each other—one allegedly in the pay of the CV, the other in support of the Lucas traffickers. The second, early on a Sunday morning, was more of a suicide mission than a reinvasion. Chico Rambo and four of his men got no farther than the footbridge before they were gunned down.

CV pride was severely dented by the loss of their traditional stronghold, but Furica had no plans to give up control. He set about blocking the main roads into the favela with concrete structures—wide, round tables painted with the word *"paz"* (peace). Masquerading as leisure facilities, these structures serve to restrict the access of police or potential invaders.

Furica also waged a popularity campaign in Vigário, distributing gifts to children and holding free raffles for washing machines, fridges, and the like. He re-plastered a bullet-ridden wall on the front line between the two favelas and painted it with peace symbols and the words "Welcome to Parada Geral." He dreamed of uniting the two communities under his command.

But in the months after the invasion, Vigário Geral became a ghost town. There were fewer people out and about. There was less traffic on the streets, less hustle and bustle. Houses emptied and businesses closed. Residents were edgy, scared that any perceived association with the new occupying force might bring reprisals should the CV return.

A friend from the accounts department at AfroReggae described life under the new regime like this: "The other day I got back to Vigário at about eight. It was dark and the light in front of my house wasn't working, so I checked the bulb and found it had come loose. The next day when I got home the light was still off, so I fixed it, thinking I couldn't have tightened it properly. On the third day I got home and it was off again. I paused under the bulb and a trafficker appeared. He asked me not to interfere with the light. My house is on the road facing the footbridge and they like to keep watch from my doorstep. What can I do?"

The occupation of Vigário by the Terceiro Comando meant that residents, who had nothing to do with drug trafficking but had cohabited with CV members their whole lives, now had to adjust to the rules and regulations of a new force. They were living under the constant threat of a CV attack.

Despite Furica's best efforts to win them over, most residents wanted to leave. Only the presence of AfroReggae staff and nuclei, both in Parada de Lucas and Vigário, offered any constancy and neutrality in these shifting sands. No doubt, the situation would have been much worse without AfroReggae's presence.

Naming the fallen

In the above passage, I have referred to the boss of Lucas by his name, Furica. Earlier in the book, Patrick and I avoided this after agreeing with Junior that we wouldn't refer to any active traffickers by name. But Furica was killed by police in August 2008, just more than a year after taking control of Vigário.

Furica's success turned out to be short-lived, and all the money he spent fortifying the community with obstacles, ditches, and CCTV couldn't protect him. The circumstances of his death suggest he was executed after giving himself up. Some say that he grew too big for his boots, provoking resentment among the police, others that the CV put a price on his head that was too good to resist.

Despite a power shift, Vigário Geral and Parada de Lucas remain Terceiro Comando. Rumors about a CV invasion surface from time to time, but the soldiers I have seen patrolling the streets do not look as if they will give up their prize easily.

Another faction boss mentioned in the book was also killed in 2008. The mild-mannered white guy we spoke to outside the *baile funk* in Complexo do Alemão was gunned down with his bodyguards in an ambush carried out by fellow members of the CV. His name was Tota and he was one of the top men in the favela, heading Rio's most wanted list for several years. Tota's murder was ordered by the CV hierarchy in prison, and afterward there were several days of parties to celebrate the end of his brutal reign.

Militias

In 2005, Patrick and I were aware that a favela called Rio das Pedras was said to be free of drug traffic. We heard that it was a favela predominantly populated by police, and that their presence kept the factions out.

At the time, news articles began to appear, documenting the growth of paramilitary groups called *milícia*. These groups were moving into areas dominated by factions and clearing them out. This activity was principally centered in the west of the city around Rio das Pedras. Throughout 2006 and 2007, the power of these groups grew. They took over localities and imposed taxes for the provision of "security" and other social services. The membership of these *milícia* was predominantly police, ex-police, prison guards, *bombeiros* (paramedics and firemen), and politicians. Notably, in the 2006 national elections, which, despite the corruption crisis, brought President Lula's triumphant reelection, these localities voted overwhelmingly for certain candidates sympathetic to *milícia* interests, including, for example, the former chief of Rio's civil police, Alvaro Lins.

Little political attention was paid to this phenomenon, however, until the beginning of 2008, when a team of investigative journalists documenting life in one of these favelas was captured, held hostage, and tortured by the militia. Fortunately their captors drew the line at executing them and, several weeks after their release, their newspaper, *O Dia*, ran a series of headline features about their experience. These reports in turn prompted the establishment of a parliamentary commission of investigation, headed by Marcelo Freixo, a former human-rights activist turned state deputy. The commission clinically exposed the main players and infrastructure that had supported the rise of the *milícia* and, by the end of the year, several high-ranking city officials were behind bars, including a state deputy, a city council member, and the aforementioned ex-chief of the civil police.

The commission's success offers some cause for optimism, showing that political will, with the right support, can achieve results. But there's a long way to go. Since the commission reported, Marcelo Freixo has only traveled by day, in an armored car, with a police escort he selected himself.

Most of all, the rise of the militia exemplifies the fact that favelas offer potential income far beyond the drug trade. Because these communities sit outside the city proper, many of the services supplied to them are also informal and, therefore, semilegal at best. Whether it's the people providing electricity, cable TV, or even taxi services in the favela, the illicit nature of these services leaves them vulnerable to anyone with the muscle to offer "security," and this was where the *milícia* could step in. For the past twenty-five years, the favelas' social problems have been consistently characterized by the equation "cops multiplied by robbers plus drugs." However, this latest development proves that the reasons behind the battles for territorial control of these communities are, as they have always been, a lot more complex than that.

Changes for the better?

These days I live in a house situated on a hillside near the bohemian neighborhood of Santa Teresa. It's an elegant part of town overlooking Catête, located just next to a favela called Santo Amaro. For this reason, taxi drivers are sometimes reluctant to drop me at my front door. On a Friday morning in January 2009 I am at home when I hear four quick shots that sound as if they came from an automatic rifle. Marcio, the gardener, tells me that there are police occupying Santo Amaro.

Police incursions into this favela are rare. It's a small and generally quiet community of a few thousand residents. I later read that the operation was the result of complaints about *cracudos*—crack users—and their unwelcome presence in the streets of middle-class Catête at the foot of the hill. According to the newspaper, the police seize 50 kilos of marijuana, 300 rocks of crack, 100 wraps of cocaine, and arrest a trafficker named Russo.

The operation is peaceful. Those four shots I heard were the only ones fired, possibly for the benefit of the accompanying TV crew. It appears to be the latest in a series of police occupations of favelas in the Zona Sul.

Before Christmas they occupied and took over Dona Marta, a sizeable community in the Botafogo District. The state government has been quick to declare that Dona Marta is now a drug traffic–free zone and that a permanent police battalion manned by new recruits will soon be established there. On the initiative of the authorities, it has even become the first favela in Brazil to offer free Wi-Fi Internet access. Luca, a former AfroReggae staff member who lives in the favela, told me, "People are happy with the changes. So far, so good."

Earlier in this book, Patrick and I discussed the endemic lack of cohesion between the federal, state, and municipal branches of government. In 2009, however, this is finally beginning to change because the different executive spheres are not only talking to one another, but even working together. They have little choice: Rio is hosting World Cup football matches in 2014 and is currently bidding to stage the Olympics two years later. The occupation of favelas in the Zona Sul, therefore, appears to be the first step in a long-term strategy to pacify this part of the city. Does this represent light at the end of the tunnel? Perhaps. But Rio still faces many challenges, and there is none greater than police corruption.

Anecdotal evidence has its limitations. However, I do believe it's worth noting that corrupt military police have been a ubiquitous presence in every favela in which I've worked and gotten to know well. I am not simply talking about crooked cops who might occasionally show up to collect a bribe, but also a form of corruption that is directly related to the very structure of policing in these communities. In every favela, there are permanent police installations called DPOs (ostensive policing posts). Naturally, the police based in these DPOs have to drive past the drug traffickers to get to work and will sit in their uniforms at their post while the traffic goes on around them. At the very least, the simple existence of these installations in areas controlled by the factions suggests an extraordinary negligence on the part of the police. It is surely more plausible, however, to infer an altogether more sinister interpretation—that of institutional complicity between the authorities and the factions.

There is also the issue of what I call "real organized crime," best exemplified by the *jogo do bicho*—the numbers game. Although illegal, the ticket vendors can be found on every other street corner and represent the tip of a vast criminal iceberg with recognized ties to money laundering and political payoffs. It is entirely reasonable to consider the corrupt city bigwigs and *o tráfico*—or, if you like, "disorganized crime"—as in a codependent situation. The traffickers need dishonest officials to look the other way, dishonest officials need the traffic for the revenue it generates and, all too frequently, to distract public attention from their own nefarious activities. Personally, I know of two recent, high-profile assassinations that were attributed to factions by the media. However, reliable sources tell me that these murders were, in fact, carried out for the specific purpose of concealing official corruption.

To my skeptical eye, therefore, significant change in Rio remains a distant aspiration. But AfroReggae continues to occupy a crucial position in the life of the city. The popularity of the institution combined with Junior's unique ability to engage with people from all levels and backgrounds enables AfroReggae to bridge gaps between government, business, and community leaders in a way that no other organization can match. Consequently, AfroReggae has launched numerous initiatives that have improved the lives of favela residents. The quality of the service delivered to the young people who attend the nuclei is constantly improving, and AfroReggae has recently added a monthly magazine, a TV show, and several radio programs to its portfolio of achievements.

Of the former traffickers Patrick and I interviewed, some two-thirds have successfully stayed away from a life of crime.

West London to Colombia

During AfroReggae's first tour of the UK, Junior attended an event at a small nightclub in West London to answer some questions about the organization's work. One woman asked him what he thought drug users had to do with the situation in Rio. "Half the people in this room are probably cocaine users," she added. While her assessment of the audience that night was almost certainly wide of the mark, it was not an unreasonable estimation of wider London club culture. Junior said he didn't have an opinion on the rights and wrongs of individual drug use, but that users should be aware that their taste for cocaine helped to finance a bloodbath.

I remembered this exchange a year later, when Junior and I touched down with a camera crew at a small airport in Apartadó, in Antioquia, northern Colombia. AfroReggae had won a grant to travel to the country. Successful in reducing homicide figures, Colombian cities were being touted as potential models for Rio and we were there to investigate.

We were told time and again that it is impossible to remain neutral in the context of the Colombian conflict. In rural areas peasants are considered "guerrilla" or "paramilitary," according to whoever controls their locality. If any of the civilian population are not prepared to accept the rule of the occupying force, they have no choice but to leave and join the hundreds of thousands of internally displaced who have flooded into the cities over the last twenty-five years. But, if they stay, they risk being considered supporters of whichever group controls their land and thus drawn into the conflict. This is, of course, precisely the same process by which favela dwellers in Rio come to be confused with drug traffickers.

Despite the potential danger, however, there is a community in Colombia that has declared itself neutral. To this day, the

Comunidad de Paz de San José de Apartadó (Peace Community of San José de Apartadó) has resisted all attempts by different groups to terrorize its population or drive them from their land; this despite the fact that Apartadó lies in an area that grants access to Panama and is therefore of significant value to those vying for control of the drug routes.

In San José, one of the first things you come across is a hand-painted sign that reads as follows:

THE COMMUNITY FREELY

- PARTICIPATES IN COMMUNITY WORK.
- SAYS NO TO INJUSTICE AND IMPUNITY.
- DOES NOT PARTICIPATE IN THE WAR DIRECTLY OR INDIRECTLY, NOR IS IT ARMED.
- DOES NOT MANIPULATE OR PASS ON INFORMATION TO ANY OF THE SIDES.

It was reading this sign that specifically made me recall the comments made to Junior at that nightclub in London. Here we were at the very beginning of the supply chain that led all the way to countless restrooms in countless bars in countless Western cities, and yet throughout the world that chain remains as invisible as it is corrosive. We spent the day in Apartadó listening to community leaders describe their struggle. These conversations reduced some of our team to tears.

Back in Rio we wrote about our experiences and produced a documentary. Word of the peace community reached Reginaldo, a community leader in the Complexo do Alemão. He raised the subject in a meeting. He wanted to know if we could turn Alemão into a neutral zone, too. "Here we live in what is effectively the largest semi-open prison regime in the world," he said. "Our right to come and go is monitored and restricted at all times. Why can't we declare ourselves neutral, just like the Colombians you met?"

For the moment, such a fanciful dream must remain just that. But it is by no means fanciful to suggest that Reginaldo was expressing one of the most important freedoms that Afro-Reggae facilitates—the freedom to have precisely these dreams.

Providência

One wet, gray afternoon in December 2007, I accompany a French photographer to Alemão. Deep in the favela, he takes a photo of a boy flying a kite. The grainy black-and-white image of smudged skies, the kite bobbing above endless stacks of matchbox houses, becomes a favorite. The photographer's name is JR.

JR is neither photojournalist nor art photographer; rather, he uses the medium as part of a process he calls "artivism" (artistic activism). He takes portraits using a lens that necessitates proximity, so that photographer and subject are forced into one another's personal space. Then he pastes enormous prints of the portraits in public spaces, often without authorization, for all to see and interpret as they wish. JR began his work in the Paris Métro system, but has since taken it to Palestine, Sudan, and beyond.

In July 2008, I receive an e-mail from JR. He wants to bring a project he is working on to Rio. Can I help? His plan is to take portraits of women in a favela and stick those same enormous prints, wallpaper-style, to the sides of houses. He will create a wall of faces and eyes on the side of a hill overlooking the city. It is part of a worldwide project that has already taken him to Liberia and Sierra Leone. I tell him I'll see what I can do.

I consider potential communities for the undertaking. Vigário Geral is flat and therefore out of the question. What about Alemão? JR rejects it as too big and too far from the city center. Can't we find somewhere that overlooks both the city and the sea? We consider Cantagalo, which is certainly a possibility. However, Cantagalo is relatively privileged, located as it is near the beach and the heady attractions of Ipanema. Besides, it is already home to a number of thriving social projects and we might not make the impact JR is looking for.

In 2005, Patrick and I had asked Junior whether it would be possible to visit Providência, the first recognized favela that was occupied by the Canudos veterans more than a century ago, which stands on the hill above the port. Not a good idea, he said. Even a man of Junior's influence and stature has to be realistic about the inherent dangers of certain communities.

Nonetheless, for JR's purposes, Providência is the ideal location. It sits just behind Central, the station that brings in commuters from the Baixada Fluminense. On the other side it commands a view over the ring road, the Zona Norte, the port, and Guanabara Bay. It is surely the most visible of all Rio's invisible communities. Unfortunately, I can't find anyone who might be able to give us access and, with JR's arrival imminent, I'm running out of ideas.

I switch on the TV to see a newscast of angry scenes of demonstrating favela residents. Soldiers are firing shots into the air. This is Providência. The army has occupied the community for several months to provide security for an initiative to rebuild houses within the favela. It is the pet project of a federal senator, and it had been unfolding without incident. Now, however, the residents are having a revolt. It turns out that some soldiers abducted three local youths and, for no better reason than spite, handed them over to traffickers from Mineira, a community run by a rival faction. Later, the boys' body parts were found in a garbage dump. Providência is a close-knit community, and it unites in grief. Residents take down the Brazilian flag, which had been flown by the army at the hill's highest point. The families of the three victims are guests of honor at AfroReggae's fifteenth birthday party, and it is for this macabre reason that I soon get to visit the hill after all and present JR's proposal to community leaders.

The project goes ahead and is JR's most successful to date. People take a shine to him and his team of camera-wielding gringos from various European countries. Perhaps the undertaking helps to alleviate the communal depression felt since the murders. Either way, JR is trusted and given free rein to explore the alleyways, squares, and streets of the hill. By August he has finished and a picture of the work taken by an Agence France-Presse photographer has appeared in media worldwide. By September giant photos of the women have been exhibited in the streets of New York and London.

During the project, we discover that there is no other social initiative in Providência. If AfroReggae's work is an example of what is possible in favelas, Providência is a chilling reminder of the status quo: a forgotten community, subject to countless police invasions, political meddling, and now army occupation. It seems that everyone is at war with the city's oldest favela.

Paradoxes

Life in Rio offers numerous realities: There is Zona Sul with its beaches, "beautiful people," sushi bars, and shopping centers; Zona Norte, the lower-middle-class suburbs of hard-working residents, soul parties, samba schools, and yet more shopping centers; and, of course, there are the favelas throughout the city, buzzing with energy, noise, and o tráfico.

To move between these realities makes Rio a complicated but rewarding place to live. But the vast majority of residents

choose just one and make their lives within its boundaries.
Ironically, considering the lack of social mobility, it is often
favela residents who are most mobile geographically. However,
they know that when they leave their homes and cross the bor-
ders into the city proper, they are entering a very different
world where very different rules apply.

I have now been researching this book, on and off, for longer than I care to remember, and while details—names, places,
and allegiances—are in constant flux, the bigger picture remains
static. Furica drives the Comando Vermelho out of Vigário
Geral after twenty years of occupation. In the moment, this
feels like a radical change. But, once things settle down, it
doesn't seem so different after all—Vigário is still controlled by
an armed group and its residents still live under the despotism
of a faction. As Paulo Baia pointed out, the traffickers serve a
purpose, even if it's simply the preservation of the status quo:
Violence leads to fear, which leads to stasis; and nobody benefits but the powerful few.

I have made some good friends in Rio and some of them
live in favelas. I have come to know the Complexo do Alemão
particularly well. Sometimes I take long walks through this
enthralling city-within-a-city that rolls out over hill after hill.
In the alleyways, squares, and streets, children of every size,
shape, and color are running and shouting and fighting and
talking and playing and just hanging out.

To an outsider, perhaps the most outstanding paradox of
favela life is that, despite the horrors of the drug wars, many
of these communities are very happy places to be. Let's look at
those kids for a moment as they play in the streets—the kites,
ping-pong, marbles, and spinning tops. Let's look at their
laughter. How many authorities in Western cities, plagued with

problems of obesity and antisocial behavior, would be jealous of at least some aspects of this lifestyle?

When I first arrived in Rio, like many gringos, I was endlessly fascinated by the traffickers and their guns. Nowadays they are nothing but tragic figures to me, sloping around in the background and ruining people's lives, none more so than their own. Fortunately, nowadays, I mostly see the laughter.

People and Places

In researching this book, we had numerous conversations in many different neighborhoods of Rio de Janeiro. Rather than providing a substantial index or glossary, we felt it would be more useful to write a short list of people and places that crop up time and again for easy reference. Rio's drug wars and, indeed, its social and political landscape are ever shifting. However, what follows was correct at the time of going to press.

People:

Abacate: Former senior drug trafficker in the Amigos dos Amigos drug faction

Altair (Martins): Senior member of AfroReggae and percussionist in the AfroReggae band

Anderson (Sá): Senior member of AfroReggae and lead vocalist in the AfroReggae band

Paulo Baia: Undersecretary for Human Rights, Rio state government

Cuco: Former *dono* in the Comando Vermelho drug faction (now deceased)

Denise Dora: Program Officer, the Ford Foundation of Brazil

Luiz Erlanger: Director of Marketing at TV Globo

JB: Former senior drug trafficker in the Comando Vermelho drug faction, now senior member of AfroReggae

(José) Junior: Executive coordinator of AfroReggae

Robertinho de Lucas: Former *dono* in the Terceiro Comando
   drug faction (now deceased)

Inspector Marina Maggessi: Head of the civil police drugs
   squad in Rio

Flavio Negão: Former *dono* in the Comando Vermelho drug
   faction (now deceased)

Luiz Inácio Lula da Silva ("Lula"): President of Brazil

Luiz Eduardo Soares: Author and academic; formerly both
   Rio State Secretary and National Secretary for Public
   Security

Jailson de Souza: Director of the Observatório das Favelas do
   Rio de Janeiro, a Rio NGO

Vitor (Onofre): Coordinator of the AfroReggae *núcleo* in
   Vigário Geral

Places:

Baixada Fluminense: Working-class suburbs

Bangu: High-security Rio jail where many senior drug
   traffickers are currently imprisoned

Cantagalo: Centrally located favela where AfroReggae has a
   núcleo; controlled by Comando Vermelho

Complexo da Maré: "Suburban" complex of favelas, control
   of which is divided between the three major drug factions
   (the Comando Vermelho, the Amigos dos Amigos, and the
   Terceiro Comando)

Complexo do Alemão: "Suburban" complex of favelas
   controlled by Comando Vermelho

Ladeira dos Tabajaras: Centrally located favela controlled by Comando Vermelho

Parada de Lucas: Suburban favela where AfroReggae has a *núcleo*; engaged in a twenty-year-old war with its neighbor, Vigário Geral; controlled by Terceiro Comando

Ramos: Working-class suburb

Rocinha: Centrally located favela controlled by Amigos dos Amigos

Vidigal: Centrally located favela controlled by Amigos dos Amigos

Vigário Geral: Suburban favela where AfroReggae established its first *núcleo*; engaged in a twenty-year-old war with its neighbor, Parada de Lucas; formerly controlled by Comando Vermelho, now controlled by Terceiro Comando

Vila Vintém: Suburban favela controlled by Amigos dos Amigos

We also make repeated reference to the Zona Sul ("the South Zone") and the *asfalto* (literally "the asphalt") as well as neighborhoods such as Leblon, Ipanema, Glória, Barra da Tijuca, Lagoa, and Copacabana. Occasionally these places are referred to specifically but often these terms are used generically, both by others and ourselves, to distinguish middle-class/wealthy areas from working-class/favela communities.

Further Information

Books (nonfiction):

Amnesty International, *Rio de Janeiro 2003: Candelária and Vigário Geral 10 years on*, AMR, 2003.

Amnesty International, *They Come in Shooting: Policing Socially Excluded Communities*, AMR, 2005.

Caco Barcellos, *Abusado*, Editora Record, 2003.

Vera Malaguti Batista, *O Medo na Cidade do Rio de Janeiro*, Editora Revan, 2003.

Luke Dowdney, *Children of the Drug Trade*, 7 Letras, 2003.

José Junior, *Da Favela para o Mundo*, Takano Editoria, 2003.

Levine & Crocitti (eds.), *The Brazil Reader*, London, Latin America Bureau, 1999.

Darcy Ribeiro, *O Povo Brasileiro*, Companhia das Letras, 1995.

Jorge da Silva, *Violência e Identidade Social: Um Estudo Comparativo sobre a atuação policial em duas comunidades no Rio de Janeiro*, Universidade do Estado do Rio de Janeiro, 2005.

William da Silva Lima, *Quatrocentos Contra Um*, ISER, 1991.

Luiz Eduardo Soares, *Meu Cassaco de General*, Companhia das Letras, 2000.

Luiz Eduardo Soares/MV Bill/Celso Athayde, *Cabeça de Porco*, Objetiva, 2005.

Drauzio Varella, Ivaldo Bertazzo, and Paola Berenstein Jacques, *Maré: Vida na Favela*, Casa da Palavra, 2002.

Zuenir Ventura, *Cidade Partida*, Companhia das Letras, 1994.

Books (fiction):

Ivan Angêlo, *A Casa de Vidro*, Livraria Cultura Editora, 1979.

Paulo Lins, *Cidade de Deus*, Companhia das Letras, 1997 (filmed as *City of God*).

Patrícia Melo, *O Matador* (published in English as *The Killer*), Companhia das Letras, 1995.

Patrícia Melo, *Inferno* (published in English as *Inferno*), Companhia das Letras, 2000.

José Carlos Oliveira, *Terror e Êxtase*, Ediouro, 2005.

Films/Television:

Cidade de Deus (*City of God*), directed by Fernando Meirelles and Kátia Lund, 2002.

Notícias de Uma Guerra Particular (*News from a Private War*), directed by Kátia Lund and João Moreira Salles, 1999.

Cidade dos Homens (*City of Men*), television series produced by TV Globo and O2 Films, 2002.

Favela Rising, directed by Jeff Zimbalist and Matt Mochary, 2005.

Tropa de Elite (Elite Squad), directed by José Padilha, 2007.

Cidade dos Homens (City of Men), directed by Paulo Morelli, 2007.

Audio:

Mr. Bongo, *Slam Dunk Presents Funk Carioca* (LP), 2004, *Favela Uprising* (LP), 2007.